KICKED INTO TOUCH

Kicked into Touch

AN AUTOBIOGRAPHY

Paul Thorburn

Stanley Paul
London Sydney Auckland Johannesburg

To Kelly and the new arrival,
due on publication day

Stanley Paul & Co. Ltd
An imprint of Random Century Group
20 Vauxhall Bridge Road, London SW1V 2SA

Random Century Australia (Pty) Ltd
20 Alfred Street, Milsons Point, Sydney 2061

Random Century New Zealand Limited
PO Box 40–086, Glenfield, Auckland 10

Century Hutchinson South Africa (Pty) Ltd
PO Box 337, Bergvlei 2012, South Africa

First published 1992

Set in Baskerville by Raven Typesetters, Ellesmere Port

Printed and bound in Great Britain by
Mackays of Chatham PLC, Chatham, Kent

A catalogue record of this book is available from the British Library

ISBN 0–09–174967–0

Contents

	Acknowledgements	vii
1	Tears of a Clown	1
2	Neath	17
3	Expelled	33
4	"Scum of the Earth" and Other Regrettable Sayings	43
5	Helicopters, Resignations, QCs and the Inland Revenue	54
6	Getting a Kick Out of the Game	73
7	"Get Your Passport"	85
8	The Big, the Small and the Talented	104
9	An International Season for Wales '91	120
10	Down (Under) and Out	136
11	My Way	151
12	World Cup '91	169
	International Career Record	181

Acknowledgements

Writing a book has been a new experience which has tested the tolerance levels of those close to me. I am indebted to Ann for her understanding, Kelly for the awakening hours and the family for their support and prompting the odd memory. To Neath Rugby Club and the Welsh Rugby Union a general thank you, and to rugby supporters all over the world, may the next game be the best one.

Much of the book was written in the offices of Rugby Vision Ltd opposite the Arms Park in Cardiff, and my thanks there to Lesley, Jill and Sera for typing the scripts and the welcome of a port during the occasional storm.

Thanks too to the suppliers of the photographs: John Harris, David Purchase, Sian Trembarth, Elwyn White, Colorsport, *Western Mail and Echo, Sunday Times* and Hills Welsh Press.

And the final word to Martyn Williams, friend, colleague and rugby fanatic – thank you.

Tears of a Clown

The journalist was outraged. "I mean to say," he sputtered, "what the hell is the captain of Wales doing crying his eyes out before a match, what?" He went on to tell his fellow scribes that what was needed by Wales was not a nervous, whimpering, emotional wreck but a man who could stand four-square to his responsibilities. "I suppose Kleenex will be the next match sponsors." And away he went into the night, amused at his own humour. For a nation which has had to depend so much on emotion to gain credibility on the rugby-playing fields, it will not do to show such weakness.

The Thorburns, let me tell you, are a crying shame then. I've never known a family so painfully emotional and with such little regard for hiding their feelings. I cried before an international match because the emotion of the day had got to me. It wasn't the first time, and anyone who has shared a dressing room with me will testify that no matter how tight-lipped I try to be, a tear is never far away. I only wish I'd made the fortune that Paul Gascoigne collected after shedding his tears of joy in the World Cup.

It is a very close family, but that is not to say that it has always been friendly. The three brothers are as competitive as any trio, and the number of fights we've had are too numerous to mention. To lose a game of tennis, cards, or anything else for that matter against either of them has devastating consequences. I'll hear about it for months on end.

Neil, my eldest brother, is the intellect of the trio, and a dentist in the RAF; Andrew, the middle one, is the sensitive brother, or so my mother insists; and I'm the quiet runt of the Thorburn litter.

I could not have wished for a better upbringing: manners and values were drummed into us from a very early age. My mother, Pauline, was a teacher and a keen sportswoman who had played hockey at county level and tennis for the University of Wales. Dad was in the RAF, moving from one base to another as a group captain in administration . He was posted in March 1962 and I entered the world when mother had joined him at Headquarters RAF Germany at Rheindahlen. He, too, was sports-mad and had played rugby for Cardiff Athletic, a club still close to his heart; but his change of allegiance was forced upon him, and those who take the Neath name in vain had better give themselves a fair amount of room.

The home has always been on Gower, where most of the family lived, including my grandparents. Their house became our home eventually, a large, comfortable dwelling. However, all three brothers were sent to Hereford Cathedral School because of my father's movements. Those early memories are of constantly changing addresses, phone numbers and environments. For West Germany read Norfolk, and then it was Berkshire or somewhere else. Eventually my parents settled on Gower.

I remember as an eleven-year-old accompanying my parents to an investiture at Buckingham Palace, where Dad was to accept his OBE. This event should be memorable enough, but we were at that time inevitably moving house, or from one camp to another, and my memories were of leaving, packing boxes, with my father in his No. 1 uniform and stopping for fish and chips on the way home. There have never been any pretensions: time would not allow such fanciful ideas – the family was the important element.

There were five years between us brothers, and I was always conscious of the other two being at Hereford Cathedral School when I entered as a mere green pup, a year younger than my form-mates. Andrew, especially, looked after the young ones and being far more aggressive, or protective as he would put it, looked after brother Neil as well, when the all too predictable bouts of bullying started.

2

His handling of two boys much older than him in a dorm one night is still talked about with the same reverence that I've heard old men talk about Marciano and Tommy Farr. Seniority sometimes rules in the dormitories, but the fittest survived rather than the oldest.

I detested my school at the beginning, since it meant leaving my parents' company. For two years I was home-sick and despite visiting my parents, who owned a weekend home in the area, I was not at all at peace with the world. Yet for the first time I was introduced to a whole new world of organised sport.

There had been soccer games at Wildridings Primary School in Berkshire and at Credenhill near Hereford, almost always featuring P. Thorburn at centre-forward; but this was a new and exciting awakening. The school had excellent facilities and enthusiastic masters. It was also an introduction to Rugby Union. Yet for those early years it also meant leaving home.

I can recall the very first day at school I was taken to watch Hereford United play West Ham in the Football League Cup during the afternoon, a game which Hereford won. I suppose it was a diversionary tactic by my parents, before the inevitable separation. I became a weekly boarder that night and spent the next two years tearful-eyed every time I was taken back to school by my parents after the weekends.

Now my days were determined by disciplined timetables, the rituals of morning services at the Cathedral, lessons, prep and being punished for talking by raps over the knuckles with plastic brushes and thwacks over the back-side with gym slippers. Tuck boxes collected from my parents would be devoured by Monday and, of course, there were new friends to be made. Most of all there was sport, and becoming immersed in tales of traditional rival-ries between our school and places like Llandovery, Christ's College Brecon, Millfield, Rydal and, the most detested of the lot, Belmont Abbey.

The dormitory I was to attend for those two homesick years was called No. 1 House: wooden floors, iron-framed beds and straw-filled mattresses. It sounds Dickensian, which it probably was, except you didn't really notice.

I sometimes wonder what would have happened if I'd been sent to a soccer school. I realise there wasn't much hope of that with my father bordering on the fanatical as far as rugby football was concerned. Naturally, with Neil being a first-team player on the wing and Andrew having made an impact in the middle forms, it would have been a monumental shock if I hadn't followed suit. It was tradition spelt with a capital 'T', and I was given scant opportunity of questioning the order of the day. Because of my early entry I ended up playing for teams a year older.

So I began as a scrum-half, became an outside-half and was eventually chosen as a full-back. I remember one of my first games as a first team full-back. It was ideal preparation for that Welsh tour of Australia in '91. We lost by more than a hundred points to Christ College Brecon, with future Welsh international Robert Ackerman as one of my opposite numbers.

Hereford also introduced me to professionalism and bribery – and my father was the guilty party! This was indeed a new world to ponder for a thirteen-year-old. He had walked into our changing room at school and announced, "For today's best tackle I will award a Mars bar." It was a game against Llandovery College, so I suppose he thought some extra incentive was needed. He was thoroughly told off by the games master, since Hereford, a traditional bastion, frowned on such corruption. I must have thought about that Mars bar, because I had a reasonable game. His comment afterwards will stay with me for ever.

"You'll play for Wales one day, my son," he said. But I wonder if he said the same thing to Andrew and Neil as well, after watching them. I can't recall whether I received the Mars bar.

In the fifth form I made it into the first team with brother Andrew as captain. The first match was memorable, not for our win against Hereford Colts but for Andrew's performance in the changing room beforehand. It was straight out of the Clive Rowlands' evangelical book of pre-match rugby sermons. He stood there ranting and raving about our responsibilities. We had better not let down our families,

4

our friends, the school, ourselves. I was to hear this speech recited by various people a number of times during my rugby career, but the first time was something of a cultural shock. It certainly established his authority, because our prop Mike Rumsey asked him for permission to leave the field during the game in order to go to the toilet. "Certainly not," said Andrew – and poor old Rumsey paid the consequences of his captain's inflexibility. Andrew was, and he will nod agreeably, a far better player than me at Hereford.

To look at him now, a balding, garrulous raconteur, it's difficult to imagine the fit and useful rugby player that skippered the school team. "Useful?" Andrew might say, "Useful? Listen mate, I carried you and your kind through many a battle without wincing." He did, too; and as a county cap and an England schools trialist, he could have been a quality player at senior level. But the social side of rugby held far too many attractions for Andrew.

At the drop of a hat he can recall moments of Andrew Thorburn magic. A victory over Bassaleg Grammar School which featured England's Stuart Barnes in a sevens tournament. The lecture he gave me, picking me up by my long hair when I had missed a certain try ("Do that again and I'll kick your teeth in"), or the victorious visits by South Gower RFC to the Bathampton Sevens – memorable, because few of us can remember a damn thing except a perilous journey there and back with Andrew at the wheel. They are moments to be relished or embellished, and with the counting of the years, the manner of re-telling has improved an hundredfold.

Until recently Andrew was a professional rugby tourist, knowledgeable on routes, planes and hotels. We didn't necessarily take the chosen route or stay at the appointed hotel but the "I got you there, didn't I?" motto of Andrew Thorburn tours has provided many a turn-your-hair-grey experience for those who have innocently taken part.

Sadly, the hypocrisy of the game in Wales and the continual criticism has got to him. One day he may recover his zest. I hope so. Whereas I would spend a few hours packing a kitbag in order to head for Parc des Princes, Andrew, Dad and Neil spent weeks planning their tactical advance on the rugby grounds of the Five Nations. The joke was that despite the hours of preparation and my father acting as a sort of respectable ticket tout, hardly anything went right for them.

On one trip to Ireland, Andrew had persuaded a bunch of friends and Dad to join him on one of the most economical trips ever scheduled by mankind. Tickets were sought and the ferry booked from Holyhead because Fishguard was closed. By the time they got to Dublin, the enthusiasm and energy required to look for a cheap B & B had gone entirely and in they went to the first available accommodation. "Bit posh, I thought," mused the tour leader on return, "The candelabras were a bit special and I noticed that all the Welsh alikadoos were there as well." The party had booked into the Westbury, one of Dublin's finest hotels, at £175 a night! I couldn't believe it when they phoned to tell me where they were staying. Some of my friends are still paying off the second mortgage, and I still wonder about Andrew's bar bill at the Westbury.

It was a far cry from the trip we once organised to Dublin as students: hired minibus, a route fixed for Holyhead and wine bottles from a Swansea supermarket, which were nearly empty by the time we were in Mid-Wales. I can't drink a great deal, and it shows, and I'll never forget watching some of the girls on board glugging away as I already wished I hadn't tasted a drop.

Again, the plans went astray and on the Saturday night after the traditional crawl through the city's hostelries, we simply had to find somewhere to stay. Everywhere was full, and so a few of us decided there was no alternative to sleeping in a shop doorway. Wrapped up in anything we could find, we settled down until the cold was unbearable. We wandered down towards the harbour and came across a small hotel. The nightwatchman had probably seen it all before and offered us what he could: a couch, a pillow and anything else he could muster. Little did I think that two years later, I would travel past the same hotel and shop doorway in the Welsh team bus heading for Lansdowne Road.

Those Swansea days as a student were glorious. Yet

getting there had been somewhat troublesome. My A level results from Hereford had not been brilliant, in fact pretty poor. It was a salutory lesson for me, because I had no alternative but to resit them. Rugby had been everything, and the sporting opportunities at Hereford had taken every spare moment. There had also been cricket for school and county as wicketkeeper, and a stab at acting in a few school plays.

The one activity that I had no trouble avoiding was music and to my eternal regret I used to mitch the piano lessons arranged and paid for by my parents with Mrs Huke. Rather than tickle ivories, there were balls to be kicked in yards and imaginary games to be played for my then favourite football team Chelsea. I told them that I had no wish to stay at the school, but I might be persuaded if the piano lessons ceased. When I have watched the likes of our Welsh players, Adrian Davies and Ian Jones, both accomplished musicians, entertain us on tour, it has been a case of guilt, envy and shame about those mitching lunch-times. Anyway, like Andrew and Neil, I am tone-deaf, a defect which also affects my father but we haven't been brave enough to tell him. Since we have always had a piano at home and good sing songs at Xmas – it's always Mum who plays. Academic subjects had taken a poor second place to sport and music a distant third.

Andrew had moved on to Swansea to take a degree in socialising with a little academic work thrown in, so I registered at Tŷ Coch Technical college in Swansea. The family house inherited from my grandparents on Gower was empty, which meant that Andrew and I became temporary landlords.

The disappointment of my academic results at Hereford convinced me, at least temporarily, that there was more to life than just sport, so for six months I concentrated on achieving satisfactory grades. Somehow a measure of credibility was achieved and with a little help from Phil King, a lecturer at Swansea, and brother Andrew, I entered University College, Swansea, on a four-year course.

I am no academic, more of a plodder, and there were now countless attractions including Rugby Union with the

University. This, I suppose was the first introduction into that dark Celtic world of Welsh rugby. First, there was South Gower RFC which was totally eccentric and hugely entertaining. South Gower were a junior club in the Swansea area, a team devoted to the enjoyment of the game. My first game featured a bugler who would blow every time he thought a move of South Gower warranted applause. A real attacking move would induce a shaky rendering of "Charge of the Light Brigade".

Unfortunately, the first game was lost, so our musician friend gave us a blast of the "Last Post" as we headed for the showers. I also remember an all-embracing tackle from a Waunarlwydd prop during a cup game which should have told me to leave the game alone. It was one of those "if you come this way again I'll really hurt you" tackles. You tend to remember them.

Soon though, the appeal of playing for South Gower gave way to more serious challenges. This was the structured world of student rugby at University College, Swansea, and a professional coach in Stan Addicott. This was another plane of operation. It was a difficult game. Tactics had to be absorbed, fitness levels attained and Swansea University's proud UAU record defended. All this, and socialising too.

Once we went as far as the UAU semi-finals, only to be beaten by Nottingham, skippered by England hooker, Brian Moore. It wasn't particularly noteworthy but on the way back I noticed a black-haired student from Northern Ireland. I was drinking a flagon of cider at the time, drowning sorrows on the homeward bound bus, so I must have appeared to be a bit of a lout. Her name was Ann, she agrees with my observation, but now she's my wife and mother of Kelly, our daughter.

Life at the Gower home was marvellous. We had other students staying there, but as custodians Andrew and I had all the comforts at our disposal. We didn't always get on. There were fights, but the aggro only lasted a few moments before brotherly peace was restored.

Andrew was there when I scored my first "try" for Wales. Both of us had travelled to watch Wales play France at the Arms Park. We'd met my father at the Royal Hotel before the match and returned there after watching a Welsh victory. There's little doubt that an unhealthy amount of beer or whatever had been consumed, since I unashamedly fell in love with the barmaid, who in turn had taken a liking to the beret I was wearing. She took the beret and I began helping myself to all sorts of things behind the bar including a large silver ice bucket.

The time came to leave my father, since Andrew and I were both returning to Gower. Around the corner were the dark shadows of the Arms Park. The stadium invited us in, or so we thought. We could without too much trouble find an entrance and fulfil a dream. The gates, however, had long been closed and . . . yes we did.

Now, what really happened has been lost in the artful telling of the story. We climbed over the high fences near the Cardiff County Club and through Block K – and suddenly the Thorburns were practising passing movements with an ice bucket on the famous pitch. I scored a try in the corner, better than any try ever scored at the Arms Park. The silence of the night became a mighty roar, though I can't remember taking the conversion. What I do remember is trying to get the clock off the scoreboard with Andrew underneath holding me up like a good supporting prop in a line-out. The clock remained out of reach and I doubt whether we would have been able to budge it. The sign for Block K with "Cardiff Arms Park" written on it looked far more vulnerable. It was a trophy worth having and suddenly it was on its way to Gowerton, or so we thought.

Our joy was shortlived, since we suddenly noticed a blue flashing light near the entrance. From the shadows emerged one of Her Majesty's officers in blue. It wasn't exactly "Evening, all", more like "And where do you think you two are going with that sign?"

You really do come up with some bright answers under the influence. We told him we'd found it.

"Put it back, then, where you found it," said the policeman, as we shuffled back towards the Arms Park, very grateful at not being asked to accompany our Westgate Street mate down to the "nick".

We hurried towards Cardiff station, lest the men in blue should have a change of heart, and caught the Swansea train. Naturally we slept, exhausted by the tries we had scored, and even after swapping trains at Swansea (which you have to do in order to get to Gowerton), we slept again. As the train was pulling out of Gowerton, I woke up and shouted at Andrew, who was lost to the world. I jumped out of the moving train and Andrew followed. The door swung open, which sent the guard into a rage at having to halt the train. We didn't bother to look back, since one warning had been enough. Two in a single evening was pushing it a bit.

We were both far too exhilarated to rationalise anything, and the competitive urge returned. I challenged Andrew to a race. He tripped, cut himself and ripped his shirt and jacket. He became incensed and gave chase, storming into the house, head-butting the sideboard and wardrobe. It was a frightening sight, and I stayed shaking under the sheets fully clothed. Life with Andrew was never dull, a fight one minute and a curry together the next.

During my international days there is little doubt that my father, Neil and Andrew had the better time. "What am I going to do for tickets, now that you've retired?" he has asked on more than one occasion. He would sit there on a Monday night before a game with Tipp-Ex in hand crossing off lists of who was going and who was not. Somehow we managed to find tickets for everyone but the phone bill was astronomical. Finding tickets now will be that much harder.

After I had announced my retirement my other brother Neil was far more direct. "Best thing you've ever done," he phoned from his base in Cambridge. He knew what it had been like and wanted to lend support.

Meanwhile my mother would always be ready for the emergencies. She would provide a late-night lasagne or help out as an emergency driver, and worry until the tribe had returned in one piece. Though she didn't know what tribulations had been confronted, I think she had a shrewd idea. She has seen it all, including a midnight drive from Gower to Cardiff to pick up the family car from the police after it had been pinched twice after an international. That would have been enough drama for a family but I think after all the phone calls and the police involvement and the eventual early morning arrival at home, we all sat down to watch a video of the game which was now a distant memory after the trauma of the twice stolen car. That she put up with it all speaks volumes for her tolerance.

It saddens me to say that my mother gave up watching rugby because of the abuse hurled at me, not only at games but through the media. Newspapers after a while were avoided. There was no enjoyment in it for her any more.

My parents and Andrew travelled to New Zealand for the World Cup, but whereas Dad and my brother would watch every single move, my mother wandered around the surrounding streets of the stadium during the game, hoping that I would come through unscathed. The surburban gardens around Ballymore Park in Brisbane were a safer haven than the uncompromising comments of the terraces. It wasn't always thus, because she was once passed down the crowd at Cardiff after fainting, and she was hit on the head by a cushion at Twickenham. That latter incident sent my father into the stand looking for the culprit with nothing less than grievous bodily harm in mind.

This, I hasten to add, happened well before I started playing. It proves, though, that my mother would have enjoyed watching the game, especially since she eventually had a personal interest and pride in such events. To be denied that pleasure, merely because of some ignorant and loutish comments, says a great deal about the "ruffians' game played by gentlemen". The Gnoll was bad enough, the Arms Park was worse. My mother would prefer a drive in the country with a close relative to watching me play on television. To her it was the homecoming that was important and the family post-mortem of all the incidents that had happened. Invariably what had happened on the field took second place to the antics of Dad, Andrew and Neil.

It was my mother who left the most critical of messages

on my answerphone after the infamous England game. To the outside world she was one hundred per cent behind us all; within the four walls she ruled with firm and disciplined authority, insisting on courtesy and dignity. She has never become immune to the criticism. Whoever does? There was a time when she'd quietly put pen to paper and write a response to whoever had been critical. I haven't been privy to the number of letters written, but my suspicions tell me that quite a few of Wales' learned gentlemen of the press have had their birthright questioned. It was a vent for her frustration, because as all parents who have been in a similar position will vouch, there is no defence against the so-called authoritative opinions of the daily columns. The letters drew little response, but I knew how much it worried her. She was angered by my antics after the England game at Cardiff, and it took time to forgive. She has always asked me to be courteous, though she suspects that there are few who deserve such privileges and fewer who return the compliment.

Perhaps it will one day dawn on the loud-mouths and the uncouth that players have families who have no defence against the prejudices of the highly paid self-appointed critics. My mother wrote a poem once and had it published in the *South Wales Evening Post*:

ODE TO A SON

"Crucify him! Crucify him!" cried press and media
A mindless mob, wild with hysteria.
The one-time greats joined in the shout,
"Out with Thorburn! Out! Out! Out!"
"But why?" asked the voice of Reason. "Why?
He has done no wrong. He should not die."
"Crucify him! Crucify him", from Edwards, John, Price.
The pleas of mercy cut no ice.
"But why?" asked the voice of Balance. "Why?
He has done no wrong, so why, why, why?"
"Crucify! Crucify! Someone has to pay
For the Welsh defeat on Grand Slam Day."
"But he has worn his Welsh shirt with pride,

Distinction, honour, humility, dignity," Reason cried.
"Is it not enough that he the Triple Crown gained
When all thoughts of victory ebbed and waned.
Remember the World Cup kick down-under
When all the crowd look on in wonder."
But pleas for mercy fell on deaf ears.
Reason and Balance realised their worst fears.
The typewriters rang, the presses rolled,
These men were determined, papers had to be sold.
And so Paul Thorburn has been made to bear
Alone, unsung, with no-one to share
The blame for defeat – the others went free!
They have their scapegoat; it's plain to see.
Is this, then, the price paid for glory and fame,
Perhaps we should remember it's only a game
Where all players go out to do their best
Whatever the outcome, with zeal and zest.
We all claim to loathe injustice and hurt
Yet you have done just that to the Number 15 shirt.
Shame on you all, you have dishonoured our Nation.
You have abused power, rank and station.
As you sat cushioned in your ivory towers
Free from all criticism and abusive showers.
It is time for truth and honest reporting.
About this young man who is loyal and sporting,
Who has always given of his best
Whatever the pressures, when put to the test.
You have all forgotten one simple rule –
Power corrupts, it's an evil tool.
Press Power is worse; for it seeks to destroy
All human dignity, hopes and joy.
But Thorburn, like the Phoenix, will rise
With honour and dignity, which we all prize,
And take his place in the Hall of Fame.
Well done, young man, you played the game!

I doubt whether I would have survived as long as I did
without my parents' support. It was always there and never
to be questioned. Perhaps my father was too supportive at
times. At the final whistle he would have summed up a

13

game, and despite convincing arguments to the contrary, that would be "the match report". If a journalist happened to agree with that account, then he was classed as a good observer of the game. I am convinced he saw no other individual on the field and we've often had arguments when he's been far too dismissive of other players. Ann, my wife, tends to be the same, especially if another full-back is mentioned in conversation. The defences immediately go up, and since attack is the best form of defence, the innocent are guilty without fair trial or hearing. Mind you, I'm a little like that, too.

Andrew and Neil are a shade more objective during daylight hours. Like the proverbial vampires they, too, have their moments of intense inflexibility. They enjoy the occasion. Andrew has this thing about getting dressed up in zany costumes, and to his credit has managed to persuade others to do likewise. On a trip to Scotland he and two others dressed up as the Three Musketeers, sweltering in stage costumes through the streets of Edinburgh. Politely, he was asked to remove his hat when he sat down in the Murrayfield stand. Neil, who like my father has travelled around the RAF bases, has gone to extraordinary lengths to watch me play.

Since he's a dentist with the RAF, he's quite friendly with the air sea rescue crews. It always amazed me how the RAF Chivenor boys just happened to be landing "a patient" at the University Hospital of Wales pad on the morning of an international, and just happened to be in the vicinity of Sophia Gardens, half a mile away from the Arms Park at the final whistle. Neil, as their only patient-passenger, would be there but part of the bargain was that he had to volunteer as a guinea pig on their sea drops near the Welsh coastline. I suppose his helicopter flights into Cardiff were legitimate, or were they?

When I won my first cap in Paris, Neil travelled over-night by train from a camp in Bavaria and arrived on the point of exhaustion. No matter, it was international week-end and tiredness is part and parcel of the act. No use arriving home looking as if you've had an enjoyable holiday. Being dishevelled and without sleep is the stamp of

14

"having been there". We hadn't quite sorted out the ticket allocation and it was left to me to get a ticket to Neil at Parc des Princes. We knew it wasn't going to be easy and elaborate efforts were made by the Thorburn ground crew to establish exactly which entrance was being used by the Welsh team bus.

I'm told that my father's verbal exclamations in achieving pole position at the gate where the bus was due to arrive would have made many a French maid blush. He won't take 'no' for an answer and did his group-captain bit with a machine-gun-carrying gendarme. How they managed to get through I'll never know, but as the bus was moving into the Stadium, I threw Neil's ticket out through the window, which prompted a mad family scramble, lest some Frenchman should think it was his lucky day.

I don't know what else happened to our lot that weekend but the whole Paris commotion was captured on film by Neil, using my parents' camera. It would have been splendid to sit back and go through what must have been another memorable episode of the Thorburns on tour, but Neil, with Bavarian tiredness and French plonk undoubtedly to blame, threw the camera with film inside under a Paris truck, and that was that. "My parents deserve a better camera than that," he told the amazed ensemble, so we have no record of that famous Paris weekend. Perhaps it's just as well: for Andrew, when asked how Ann and I were getting on, told the French millionaire, Lucien Piquet (in his table d'hôte French), that Ann had me by the balls. A Frenchman nearby completely misunderstood Andrew's statement, but took a lot of interest in his whereabouts for the remainder of the evening.

The tales are told, and Mother sometimes winces. Naturally, we've had to change a few names to protect the guilty. Invariably, they have been boisterous events of young men. We will laugh at them again when the clan gather. Andrew will tell you yarns and the rest of us will punctuate with tactful corrections. The man who once tried to get Nigel Starmer-Smith to send a "Best wishes" message to a friend during his World Cup commentaries is the life and soul of any gathering.

At the World Cup, Andrew and I, on a day off from training, went with the rest of the squad to the Gold Coast in Australia. It was one of the highlights of that demanding competition. After a good session at one of the local bars, we stupidly decided to go for a quick swim. We didn't have any swimwear, so in we went as Mother Nature intended. Unknown to us, Gareth Roberts, the Welsh flanker, and a neighbour of mine, was watching all of this and stole our clothes.

We saw him and gave chase, or at least I did. Andrew was not, by then, the fit man he used to be. I followed Gareth all the way up the beach, along the promenade and into a McDonalds. I stood there naked, looking for Gareth. Andrew arrived and was not slow with the quote. "That's the smallest Big Mac around here!"

2

Neath

It is match day at the Gnoll, home of Neath.

We call it the "pleasure dome" for opponents, since few visiting teams have been successful there in recent years. Down in the changing rooms, we find a subterranean, secretive, murky world of three changing rooms which has been fashioned, not designed, by decades of black-vested warriors. I often thought the Neath changing rooms were more akin to pithead baths than the facilities of a successful rugby club. Understandable perhaps, since the Neath team over the years has boasted miners, steelworkers and hard men. There's the hint of hard labour all around you. The rooms were recently painted and refurbished but a coat of paint will never erase those first memories of Neath's dark rugby parlours.

"THIS IS THE GNOLL" says the fading plaque above the entrance. It was placed there, a direct copy of the one at Anfield, by Brian Thomas, known as "Twmws", "Guru" or "Ayatollah" – a name which he hates, incidentally. Another of his plaques reads "No pain – No gain". Brian has yet to appear. The early and eager individuals have already dumped their bags on the wooden benches and the room begins to fill with idle chatter.

The economy of Wales has changed dramatically over the past decade. There are few miners around, the supply of steelworkers has almost disappeared; yet Neath has resisted change as best it can in some directions but has been revolutionary in others.

When Brian Thomas took over at the club in the early 80s, with Ron Waldron and Glen Ball as able lieutenants,

17

mediocrity reigned. Seventy-two players had been used in the '82 season. The club had recorded its first win in eight years over neighbours Aberavon, and success in cup and unofficial championship tables were distant memories. Drastic surgery was required.

I doubt whether the Neath committee, in asking Brian to implement a recovery plan, could ever have anticipated what was going to happen in the next five years. Nor could they have anticipated a few years later paying Brian £36,000 a year on a ten-year contract for his expertise. He used those early formative years to implement and develop his managerial policies. He has that blotting-paper kind of mind for absorbing detail and knowing when to implement action. Those who stand in his way are not around for long. The first casualty was the captain, Peter Rawlins, who disagreed with selection policy. He left without ceremony. Elgan Rees, the club's only international at that time, took over.

"Twmws" then squeezed his impressive frame into his car and went searching for talent, or "raw men" as he would put it. Not for him the schoolboys or youth players who had been recognised and capped at various levels. He would look at the reserve or replacement lists, his argument being that they would be hungrier for success. The car, or sometimes a motor-bike, headed towards West Wales, past Stradey Park, home of Llanelli, to the farms of Dyfed. There Brian was to find a rich vein of talent: young men who toiled with heavy machinery and handled livestock by day and had uncomplicated philosophies towards life.

Brian has little time for time-wasters or for rugby bureaucrats, and his appreciative thoughts on the WRU would not fill the side of a matchbox. His questions, however couched, are full of mischief for the unsuspecting individual. That is why he appreciates the uncomplicated attitude and approach of his players and coaching staff. To try to be clever is to invite trouble. To be devious would invite disaster.

His intentions were always honourable when dealing with players. I do not know anything of his business dealings, though I suspect that he is fairly astute, especi-

18

ally when he's not getting his own way. A wry grin appears and a chortle is heard when he knows he has someone in a corner. He enjoys finding fault with the press, as well, especially if there's a hint of a lucrative libel statement in the columns. Whatever money he's gained through the courts has gone to charity. It is the "Twmws" way.

To me and my wife Ann, Brian has displayed amazing generosity. He paid the travel costs for Ann and me to go to France one summer and to stay with a friend of his from his old club in Clermont Ferrand. The plan was that I could play for the club and take a break as well. All was well until we arrived in France to be housed in what I could only describe as a squatters' hole – one bulb, no hot water, peeling paint, that sort of thing. It was so bad that we spent the weekends in a tent, and I never did play for the French club because the French authorities wouldn't give me a licence. Yet Brian's intentions were good, and the "holiday" was an unforgettable experience.

If a player found himself in trouble or in some kind of a pickle, "Twmws" was always available. Unlike those responsible for the welfare of the Welsh team, the lines of communication in Neath were always open. It wasn't necessarily a matter of attention to detail, but recognition of the problems and worries which confronted players as individuals. A bereavement in the family or a birth would prompt a response. In turn, of course, this consolidated loyalty.

You can hear "Twmws" arrive. The give-away is the clatter of flip-flops or sandals on the steps. It could be a wry laugh at something he's heard, since he enjoys banter more than anything, especially if it's mischievous and quotable at a later date. Better still if it's a joke at the expense of the WRU. Suddenly his frame appears, nurtured by countless famous double-tiered curries, interspersed with publicly announced monastic diets. He is clothed in what he would term "smart casuals": an NCB jacket, large jumper and jeans struggling to defy gravity. He would defend his sartorial choice with intensity, and he only laughed when the squad decided to opt for Yves St Laurent suits in order to improve the club's image. I never once saw him on the field in either a track suit or boots, but rumour has it that a large frame was seen jogging on the perimeters of the Gnoll one evening. It could have been him, but then again it was probably the shadow of a passing cloud.

Jeremy Pugh wanders into the changing room. He is to us an Arthur Daley-type character, King of Builth Wells and an entrepreneur *par excellence*. He was the first player to be capped from Builth, and was not slow to capitalise on his fame. I have no faith in politicians, even less after Jeremy won a seat on Brecknock Council after standing as an Independent against Labour. Immediately the conversation is about deals struck during the week, whether it be to do with cars, videos, gas containers, the licensed trade or whatever. We know him to be a wealthy man; but, how can I put it, if all the deals had gone through, Jeremy would by now be chairman of the Stock Exchange and quoted on the FT Index. It's not for me to say that there is an element of embellishment in his descriptions of some of the more lucrative deals struck in Mid-Wales, let us just say that a fair amount of elasticity is required in the credibility department when Jeremy launches himself into a tale of another unsuspecting individual caught by the Pugh entrepreneurial banter. He meets his match in "Twmws".

"You're late" says the Big Man, blocking out the limited daylight filtering into the Neath changing room. Pugh thinks about protesting and pointing out how hazardous a journey he has just undertaken, but then rethinks his strategy. Pugh is always late and is the only member of the Neath squad never to have completed the fitness laps under the running coach Alan Roper. There was always an anatomical twinge which would prevent Jeremy from arriving on the field on time except when the expenses were the subject of discussion.

"Twmws" stalks the changing room exchanging insults with whoever is willing to listen. There are the quiet ones and the noisy individuals. Alan Edmunds' tongue we have always suspected was sponsored by Duracell, since it never stopped, on or off the field. Kevin Phillips and the rest of the Farmers Union of Wales brigade are quiet, always quiet. I shared a room with Kevin during the Welsh tour of Namibia and I can count on one hand how many times he opened his mouth in four weeks. The farmers, Kevin, Brian Williams and John Davies, all internationals, live in a Celtic world of their own.

When Brian Williams joined Neath, I don't think anyone understood a word he said for twelve months. I know Ann certainly didn't. He and the other two can lose themselves in a Welsh linguistic world with a few English profanities thrown in to persuade the rest of us non-Welsh speakers that they are from this planet. A drinker of unpasteurised milk and eater of fatty foods, Brian lives for his rugby and somehow manages to combine an international training schedule with the demands of milking and dairy farming.

There was a period at Neath when the committee took us to task about the number of jerseys being used. After training sessions, the jerseys were collected and counted, but invariably the figures wouldn't tally. The odd jersey would always go missing between laundry and kit basket, but someone, somewhere, was kitting out an entire squad from the Neath jersey pile.

One day I was on business in West Wales, and since I knew Brian and Kevin lived in the vicinity I decided to pay them a visit. That was fine in theory, but in practice that part of Wales is a maze of country roads, which to the outsider is a baffling experience. You could be lost for days, with or without a map. I thought I was near to Brian's farm, at least after an hour of reversing into fields and gates I had convinced myself that I was in the vicinity. Suddenly, I got lucky. Around one corner I noticed a farm labourer on top of a tractor with a Neath jersey on his back. Behind him were others kitted out in the All Black jersey, and one of them had a no. 15 on it! A half-mile further on I came across Brian, again in a Neath jersey. The mystery was solved – half the farming community in Pembrokeshire were sporting Neath jerseys. To Brian they seemed to be just the thing to wear on a cold milking morning. To the Neath treasurer, the vanishing jerseys had been a major headache, contrived or otherwise. It had been known for

21

the Neath committee to drive into West Wales to check a player's travel allowance claim.

No doubt Brian was doing a swell job in marketing the Neath jersey to the West Wales livestock. He was slightly upstaged by Kevin, who had a huge Maltese Cross printed on his car. You could never doubt their loyalty, but there were other areas which required much greater application. Now, when it came to dress sense and promoting the club image, Brian and Kevin would not immediately come to mind.

Some of the Neath boys were asked to be present at the opening of a sports shop in the town centre. Up came the Pembrokeshire lads, jeans, T-shirt and silage. They stank the place out! Just the sort of image needed by the shop to impress their new clients. As far as the lads were concerned, they had done the business by turning up – to hell with the niceties. Brian Williams, especially, wasn't one for the grand social calendar. He once fell asleep in a sponsor's bowl at a Swansea dinner.

I wouldn't want to quarrel with any of them. They are hard people who ask few favours but know exactly what is required of them. Brian, it has been argued in many quarters, does not have the build of an international prop, but there are few stronger men around and as the ripper of a ball he had few peers. His party trick, as we can all recall at Neath, was pushing his shoulder back into its socket. He missed one season through injury, and time was too short for Brian to consider missing too many matches. It was a trial game at the beginning of the season and out came the shoulder. With a toothless grimace and a few chosen Welsh profanities, in went the shoulder and off strutted Brian to the next rolling maul.

These are the men who have inherited the Neath terms of trade handed down by the blue-scarred Men in Black. There is that intensity within Welsh rugby that few people from outside understand or comprehend. Matches played against neighbours Aberavon are as competitive as any in the land. It doesn't matter what the seasonal records show before the Christmas derby begins. Everything is equal before the whistle, and woe betide a lapse in concentration.

When I first joined, players like Steve Dando, Dai

Morgan and Mike Richards frightened me stiff. Not a Christian thought between them as they relished the prospect of another afternoon of relieving frustration at the expense of the opposition. There was also Carl Gnojek, probably the smallest scrum-half I've ever played with but certainly the most competitive. To watch him go into a maul or a ruck in search of the ball was one of the Gnoll's more intriguing sights. There were men three times his size all around him, but without care for life or limb he would emerge, somewhat toothless and take them on again on the blind. Neath had a core of such individuals before the "Twmws" plan took shape. They would be needed during the interim period of rebuilding.

Ron Waldron has arrived in the changing room. Before his elevation to national coach he couldn't remember the names of any of our opponents. "That so-and-so pansy that Wales have picked" would be our only clue as to the identity of the player. To Ron it didn't matter who the opposition were, Penarth or Llanelli – the intensity was the same. There are those who have accused Ron of being blinkered in selection, favouring Neath players to the point of nepotism. There may be some justification in some instances, but at least Ron knew his players and in turn they knew what was required of them, especially when it came to fitness.

When at Neath, I don't think Ron cared a great deal about what anyone said or wrote about him; but woe betide the scribe or pundit who had a go at his players or the Neath club. He would give the same loyalty to his squad as they would to him. In that respect he had much in common with "Twmws". His speech, with impersonation provided by Phil Pugh behind his back, was virtually the same every Saturday. He would briefly analyse the opposition strengths and weaknesses, but essentially it was a reminder of each player's responsibilities and the need to do the simple things well and effectively. It mattered little which individuals he rated within the opposition ranks, since the game was more about our performance than theirs. I suspect, though, that a great deal of this was to do with his memory lapses. To single out an individual was probably tantamount to revealing that we had a weakness in our make-up, and that wasn't on. There was a single-minded approach to it all, an attitude that didn't win many friends when he was elevated to national coach.

Ron couldn't understand, or possibly wasn't able to understand, those who questioned his decisions. It was for the best, for the club or country, a dedication born out of fierce loyalty. Superficially the jibes from the media and elsewhere that he had favoured Neath players at national level, didn't bother him, yet I suspect that every time he heard or read a critical comment it hurt. He could give you the impression of taking everything in his stride, having that inner patience and tolerance of a man who has spent countless hours biding his time as a merchant seaman.

There was one exception. The days and weeks before Neath played the All Blacks at the Gnoll had all the trappings of a siege. I have never known him, at least at club level, to be so worked up. It was the ultimate test, to pit his men and mettle against the best in the world. Like Ray Prosser at Pontypool he had met the New Zealanders as a player and had never forgotten the lessons. They had been bitter ones. The match had his undivided attention for months. The same could be said about all of us. The date was 25 October 1989, but the planning in Ron's mind had begun a few years before that.

Kitted out in unfamiliar white jerseys with a black band, we had been physically and mentally prepared for our biggest test. On the strength of that performance Phil Pugh and Gareth Llewellyn were to win their first caps, but, charge as we might, the All Blacks defence held and we had to concede defeat by 26–15. The try count also favoured the All Blacks by four to one, but what impressed me was their collective coolness under pressure and their capacity to organise defences. They gave the impression that despite being under pressure they were capable of another gear of operation, whereas we were going flat out. Mistakes were made and we lost scoring opportunities. We might have won but hardly deserved to do so. It wasn't through lack of effort or the partisan baying of the crowd, but it must have been a major disappointment to Ron.

Having complimented the All Blacks for their performance, I have to say that their manners afterwards hardly
did them justice. For them to visit Neath was a huge
honour for the town and the club, and naturally they were
asked to pose and sign autographs. Some did, but others
declined and one could hardly describe them as gracious
guests. I recall Fitzpatrick, the hooker, responding to an
autograph hunter by refusing the request with the words
"Can't you wait until the end of the meal?" I know the
demands made of players are sometimes irritating, but
grace after winning was in short supply that night.

The preparation for that game had been meticulous and
the victory went to the better side. The only other occasion
when a national team played at the Gnoll also ended in
defeat, but whereas there was no disgrace in being beaten
by the All Blacks, losing to the Americans was a different
matter altogether. I was grateful to be injured.

The American Eagles were in Wales during 1987 and the
fixture against Neath was the fourth of their tour. They had
been defeated by Breconshire, Ebbw Vale and Glamorgan
Wanderers in their first three games; so Neath, as Welsh
champions and defenders of a ground record, were not
expected to have any problems with Fred Paoli's men. A
few of us were either injured or being rested for the
forthcoming international against the Americans, but
Neath's strength in depth was considered sufficient to win
the day.

How wrong can you be? On a damp Saturday afternoon,
the Eagles played the game of their lives, tackled everything
and by keeping a man out of their rucks and mauls stunted
our usual progress on the fringes. David Joseph was
disciplined by Brian Thomas for a head-butt on the
American no. 8, Brian Vizard, and we struggled in the
scrums; the whole afternoon was a Neath nightmare. The
Americans won 15–6: all in all it was a good game to miss.
Fortunately, a week later, I was able to play for Wales in a
46–0 win against the Eagles at Cardiff. What the Gnoll
match proved to Ron was that preparation for any opposition, no matter who they are, has to be exactly the same.
It may not be the inspirational stuff of other coaches or

manuals, but I doubt whether Ron has ever allowed us to underestimate the opposition after the Yanks taught us a lesson in preparation and motivation.

The banter in the Neath changing room has increased since Alan Edmunds' arrival. The excitable Edmunds tongue has launched itself into characteristic feverish activity. Paul Jackson, one of the most feared men on the Welsh forward circuit, close-shaven and at one stage sporting a pigtail, relishes the prospect of another eighty minutes of charging at the opposition. He sits motionless like a Buddhist disciple, perspiration glistening on his forehead, waiting for the "off".

"There's too much pissing about here," shouts Ron Waldron, and suddenly there is silence. A few minutes are allowed to address yourself to the task ahead. You know that the opposition will come at you in a wave of physical challenges, hoping to gain the initiative early on. It has always been the same since Neath's run of success. Fortunately, few teams have been able to sustain that early momentum. Eventually the Neath machinery has been able to weather the early punishment.

There is a profound belief in the collective will of the Neath squad. Few players arrive at the Gnoll with established reputations. It is true enough that Stuart Evans, Barry Clegg and David Pickering were international players before their Neath playing days, but the rest have emerged through the Neath drills and the structure, and under the "Twmws", Waldron and Ball management. Alan Edmunds, Allan Bateman, Chris Bridges, the Cardigan née Pembrokeshire front row, Phil Pugh, Rowland Phillips, Jeremy Pugh, Mark Jones, the Llewellyn brothers, Martyn Morris – all these are internationals who owe their allegiance to Neath and to Ron Waldron. And of course there was Jonathan Davies.

I have never forgiven Jonathan for leaving Neath. Or perhaps I should say I cannot understand a player who moves from the club which has given him the stage to develop his talents. Jonathan was picked up as an emerging and exciting outside-half, having been spotted when he played for the Welsh Districts XV and for his village club

Trimsaran. Of his ability we had no doubt, though perhaps he irritated a few of the squad who were never convinced that he was committed to the collective cause or his own. He was a match winner, and if any of us ever doubted his ability in front of what was then a world record club match attendance of 56,000 for that WRU Cup Final . . .

Jonathan had moved to Llanelli at the beginning of the season, and I had taken over the captaincy of Neath following Stuart Evans' departure to Rugby League. Pontypool and David Bishop were the champions of Welsh rugby, but the outcome of the Cup was to be resolved between ourselves and Llanelli. Jonathan's defection had caused some bitterness in Neath, although to a certain degree I can see why he wanted to play for his local first-class club. Others in the Neath camp were less tolerant. On the morning of the Cup Final Jeremy Pugh produced a "Get well" card for Jonathan and a few of the players signed it with some uncomplimentary suggestions. It was more of a "We'll get you" card than any sincere concern for his health. I didn't sign it because I thought it was rather foolish and would probably inspire Jonathan into a scarlet rage.

It did. He played us off the park with an awesome display of tactical line-kicking. Ieuan Evans scored an early try, and the grand old fighting warriors of Llanelli – May, Cornelius, Delaney and Buchanan – once again forgot their veteran tags and rose to the challenge. Yet Jonathan's contribution in a tight and hard-fought final was immense. "Black Death Caused by Scarlet Fever" said the headline banner at the Arms Park, but to this day I am convinced that the sending of the card lost us that Cup Final. I was injured eight minutes from the end as my chin caught Jonathan Griffith's boot, and the result was a sleepless night at Neath General Hospital. As I was leaving on the Sunday morning Anthony Buchanan, Llanelli's loose head prop, arrived at the hospital for attention carrying a winner's tankard! Beaming as usual from one cheek to the other, little did Anthony know that I was secretly cursing my own prop for the sending of that stupid card.

Jonathan was undoubtedly his own man, with an impish

attitude towards life. He and I enjoyed each other's company, and wherever there was mischief in the air you knew that Jonathan wasn't too far from the action. Few people got one over him, and I am delighted that he's made such an impact in Rugby League.

There was a side to Jonathan that didn't appeal to me. Occasionally he would say something without thought and it made me wonder whether he cared at all. Ann and I had gone down to the Cwmtawe Sevens tournament after Jonathan had left Neath to join Llanelli. It is a good occasion, and our main reason for going there was to see Jonathan. Llanelli were short of a player and so I approached Jonathan.

"I wouldn't mind a game if you're short," I said.

"Hey," said Jonathan. "We're not that short!"

I have remembered that remark. He probably hasn't. It just made me think.

Fortunately, by the following year's Cup Final, same place, same time and same opponents, Llanelli had lost Jonathan to Rugby League and we made no mistakes, including the sending of "Get well" cards, and won the Cup by the narrowest of margins, 14–13. It was Neath's first Cup for seventeen years, a long wait since it was a match in which Brian Thomas last wore a Neath jersey. However, the game will be remembered for the Mark Jones incident. Mark stamped on Laurence Delaney's head, and the referee Les Peard ordered him into the "sin-bin", a half-way house custodial sentence and an experiment which was eventually dispensed with by the Welsh Rugby Union. Les came under fire for not sending Mark off the field, though Mark protested his innocence by saying what he did was not intentional.

There's little doubt that Mark Jones had discipline problems. If antagonised he could erupt. The problem was that opposing players knew this. When I was captain of the club I would have a quiet word with him, the last of the players to see and counsel before taking to the field. He was enormously shy and embarrassed about his stutter. The instinct always was to withdraw, and I'm convinced that at times he could forget where he was.

Mark had no problems in motivation, since he lived for his rugby, a means of expressing himself. I can see him now, chest out, ventilating himself into another sphere of operation and into an unapproachable frame of mind. "Mark", I would tell him, "just use your head out there, don't lose it, because every ref in the country has you marked down."

Unfortunately, it was advice that he sometimes took far too literally. There were times that I thought he was a hindrance to us, giving away stupid penalties, and there were other times where he played to world-class standards. Off the field you couldn't have wished for a better ally; yet on it, he gained a reputation with other players as a dirty player. The pressure on him was enormous. There is little wonder that on occasions he lost control.

Look around the changing room once again. The awareness of what is expected of you has now heightened. Neath feared no one at the Gnoll, yet there were teams that drew more respect than others. Bath and Llanelli, for instance, were always formidable opponents. The English West Countrymen had a marvellous pack and gifted three-quarters, and a determination to succeed which was equal to our own.

I shall never forget one "Twmws" incident with Bath. There had been a seventy-odd point defeat at the Recreation Ground, but Neath were beginning to get their act together under Brian, and in the next game in the West Country we won a marvellous competitive match by 28–24. It was the day when a notice calling us "You Welsh bastards" appeared in the changing room. That got us going.

Then Brian Williams dislocated his shoulder and as he was being carried off the field, a Bath supporter shouted "You Welsh pansy!" "Twmws" located the voice in the crowd and to this day that fellow can thank his lucky stars that Brian couldn't leap over the railings, because GBH would have been one of the lesser charges against the Neath manager.

They say that Neath fans are biased and one-eyed. At least Llanelli fans will tell you that. I suppose we do have our share of the Cyclops brigade, because that is the nature of Welsh parochialism. The chants of "Neath, Neath, Neath" are no more intimidating than those heard at Stradey or Pontypool Park. What is intimidating at Neath is the close proximity of the crowd. They will tell you exactly what they think of you, but reserve special oral venom for referees. Yet they are by no means the worst supporters.

If I had to nominate the most biased and unsportsman-like crowd it would be a close-run competition between Gloucester and the touchline crowd at Maesteg Celtic. The latter is memorable for one woman and her cronies who swore and cussed at me and Neath during a cup-tie with mouths as big as shovels. Because of them, I left the ground without paying respects to the home club. I see no reason to be so venomous, and that is why I never shout or pass comment as a spectator: you never know who is standing alongside. My brother Andrew, a much travelled and staunch rugby supporter, has had enough: he cannot abide the caustic and vitriolic attacks on people who after all are human and doing their best for club and country.

The Kingsholm at Gloucester is another ground where you are so close to the spectators that you can guess their digestive or liquid intake of the day. The foul-mouthing is incredible, and after a Saturday game I once decided never to play there again. I have since relented. No doubt other players would offer some unfavourable comments about our supporters at Neath, but the humiliating and personal taunts are something every player can do without. Anonymous letters are another source of resentment.

Kevin Phillips, about to lead the team onto the field, is a man of few words. He's one of those who leads by example, taking the knocks as much as anyone and leading the charges from the front rather than being a supportive player. We've had "words" often enough on the field when Kevin pushes his way from a short penalty. Sometimes he looks around to see if I want a go at the posts, sometimes he forgets. But now he's ready for his captain's speech. It is short and to the point, just a reminder of what Neath expects on the afternoon. There may be a press cutting on

30

the wall predicting our downfall or he may remind us that a player has just become a father. Kevin tries to personalise everything. It is the Welsh way. By now, no one is mistaken. There are eighty minutes of serious activity waiting for us. It is not all doom and thunder. The two Pughs, Edmunds or the great clubman Steve Powell, are well capable of the light comment. Yet one look at the Cardigan front row will remind you that we are not about to take to the music-hall stage.

That unity has always been there as far as I am concerned. It may appear clannish to the outsider, but there are very few individuals who have played for Neath who haven't been enveloped by that united or even family approach.

I remember joining them after a few games for Ebbw Vale. Because of travel difficulties, and being at Swansea University, I tried my luck with them. I remember the first training night. Stupidly I tried to hand off Steve Powell in a friendly run-around. The next time I had the ball I was given a "welcome to Neath tackle" by Powell the milkman. I tried not to show the pain and I know that I didn't attempt anything so foolish again. Steve typifies the Neath attitude. I doubt if there's a better clubman in the country. Up at all hours with his milk rounds, he played well over a hundred consecutive games for the club in every position except lock. Perhaps I could attempt to match his loyalty to Neath, but never his drinking habits! I don't know how he does it. Four pints of lager and I am gone, whereas for the likes of Steve and a few other Neath players, four pints would merely represent an introductory course. "Play hard" would be a suitable motto for Steve, who after that tackle became a close friend.

That first season was most enjoyable because it had started on a controversial note. Neale Harris, the Neath full-back and a prolific points scorer, had joined South Wales Police. Brian Thomas claimed publicly that his player had been pinched, and such was the feeling within the Neath club that fixtures between the two sides were broken off. It didn't help matters, either, that Martyn Morris had also joined the Police. So for the new full-back,

31

whoever he might be, it was going to be a hard tussle to fill Neale's kicking role.

Fortunately, everything went well from the outset. After a baptism at Abertillery, we had a game against Cardiff, brimming with internationals, Terry Holmes, Gareth Davies, Mark Ring – the lot. We won, and I shall never forget one incident from that game. Alan Hopkins, our flanker, dislocated his shoulder and started to walk off the field. "Twmws" would have none of it and ordered Alan and his damaged shoulder to stay on. He scored the winning try in pain. Significantly, it was the start of a marvellous sequence of wins against Cardiff, who by the start of the 90s had begun to consider us as their "bogey" team. There is nothing sweeter than a victory over Cardiff, because they epitomise to me what Neath are not. When you look at the Cardiff club, with their matching shoelaces and expensive outfits, it is impossible to avoid thinking that they are, in the main, hired rugby players and not home-grown.

The points kept coming in the first season, and by the half-way stage I had captured Neale's record, and ended up scoring 438. By the end of it, I was to win my first international cap as well, in 1985. So in the light of what I have to say later, you could say that the move to Neath was one of my best career decisions.

Ron and Glen have left the changing room. Brian has long gone. The referee has been in to make his last-minute checks. It is another Saturday at the Gnoll. The visiting team have gone up the stairs and onto the field to relative silence from the crowd. The banded head of Kevin is seen by the terraced crowd and the chants of "Neath, Neath, Neath" welcome the team.

Brian Thomas watches from the terraces and exchanges banter. Ron and Glen are somewhere in the changing room area. They will remain quiet until training on Monday night. It is now up to the individual, but more importantly the collective will.

It is match day at the Gnoll.

3

Expelled

It was too good to be true. Here was this man approaching me in the bar at Newport Rugby club, whisky and water in hand, and offering me the opportunity of a lifetime. Whatever the demands of the job within the Xell company, it would give me a comfortable £25,000 salary and enough time to concentrate on my rugby. What man or beast wouldn't listen? I did, but I wish I hadn't.

A few months later I sat listening to Fraud Squad officers telling me about the activities of a certain Ray Griffiths, my employer, a man with big ideas but few principles – a cheat, as far as I'm concerned. I make no apologies for giving him so much attention in this book. It was a salutory lesson for me, and hopefully any young rugby player with ambitions will learn how gullible a prey he can be for the plausible but corrupt businessman. Promises are unkept in all walks of life; but when your entire livelihood depends on what someone has offered you, it becomes more than the nuisance of a broken promise. Other tales of his exploits have no place in this book. This is simply my personal account of my own dealings with one Ray Griffiths.

After leaving University college, Swansea, with a degree in microbiology, my primary aim was to find employment. Microbiologists were not exactly in demand in the Neath area. My first job was as salesman with a security company based in Cardiff which had the former policeman and Welsh international Arthur Rees on its board. It was comforting to know that something was coming into the house every month, but I couldn't see much future in the position, so I kept scanning the vacancy columns.

Along came a sales position with the giant pharmaceutical company Glaxo. From the first moment of visiting busy GPs and hospitals, I knew that to succeed, I would have to move to London. It would have meant sacrificing rugby for a career structure and I was too young to accommodate such serious strategies. Not having entertained any desire to cross the Severn Bridge this, too, became a burden. As one would expect from such a large organisation, although considerate, they had little understanding of the demands made on a rugby player at international level. I could appreciate their view and have no complaints about my treatment, since players at the top level have always been dependent on the goodwill of their employers. The position is even worse for the self-employed. Yet it came to a head when New Zealand were due to visit Wales, and it wasn't a match I wanted to miss.

Glaxo had arranged a conference in the United States which was to be held a few days before the All Blacks match and it was made abundantly clear that they expected me to be there and to forgo one international. I appealed, but there seemed to be little chance of persuading them that to face the All Blacks at Cardiff was just as important as all the pills I could sell for them.

My appeal went to board level. The best offer they could make was to fly me from the States a day or two before the match. Forget mental or physical preparation, which are crucial for any player, it was that arrangement or nothing at all; and, as they explained, it was the best they could do. There was a Welshman on the Glaxo board, and fortunately at the eleventh hour it was agreed that I could stay and face the New Zealanders. On reflection, after our performance at Cardiff, perhaps it would have been more charitable to insist on my presence at the conference. I knew that however justified I felt in making demands, it would only be a matter of time 'before the Glaxo people would question whether I was too much of a burden to carry. There are few companies around able to hide the luxury of having a rugby player in its workforce. I had begun to put feelers about and I'd also had a chat with the Welsh coach of the time, John Ryan.

34

The name of Ray Griffiths cropped up, and although I was aware that he was the father of Damion Griffiths, the Wales "B" wing, and the sponsor of the Welsh team to the Students World Cup in France, I knew little else about him; but the fact that he seemed to be a philanthropic rugby man was attractive. He approached me in Newport, a stocky fellow, moustached and wearing a blazer. I listened intently as he explained how his communications and computer company, Xell, wanted to expand in Wales and how he would welcome sportsmen into his company. He gave me his telephone number.

As far as I was concerned the offer was attractive and tailor-made. For the salary, which was a considerable increase on my Glaxo earnings, I would be involved in communications and sports management – I would concentrate on training in the morning and on work in the afternoon. Time off for tours or squad sessions would be no problem whatsoever, and my physical fitness programme would come under the direct supervision of the Australian, Dave Crottie. He, incidentally, had a marvellous track record in developing all manner of sportspeople, including the New York Jets and Jane Fonda. It was everything that any rugby player would want.

After our initial conversation, I phoned Griffiths and was invited to visit his company headquarters at Brunel University. Xell was housed in an annexe attached to a laboratory-style building. Perhaps I should have noticed how temporary everything appeared, but after meeting Una, his secretary, and his colleague Ivor Jones, a London Welsh committeeman, I was ready to be approached once again.

We discussed salary and job description.

"Don't worry," said Ray Griffiths, "People who work for me don't get less than £25,000."

It sounded good, and I made my way back to Wales content at last that I had a job which would benefit my rugby and please my bank manager. My father had reservations about the deal. Ann, my wife, didn't; nor did I.

A few more trips to London were arranged so that Ray Griffiths could outline in greater detail what the job involved. During these discussions he talked a great deal about how New Zealand and Australian players benefited from having job sponsors. A compulsive name-dropper, he sounded impressive. The more I listened, the more convincing he became.

The first warning shot came during those initial meetings, but there are none so blind as those who will not see. I had travelled to London to finalise matters. He invited me to lunch at the Wig and Pen Club. When he entered, it was obvious he was a regular customer since the doorman and waiters all greeted him by name. We finished our meal and the bill was brought to the table. The lunch had cost £40.

"Oh," he said, "I've left my cheque book upstairs in my coat."

"Don't worry," I said, "I'll take care of it".

I paid the bill and as soon as we got into the car, he promptly signed a cheque for £60 – the extra £20 to cover my travelling expenses. There didn't seem to be anything extraordinary about the transaction. That was, until the cheque bounced! I rang him up to explain what had happened. He was very apologetic and told me he and the company were in the process of transferring accounts, from a Scottish bank to Barclays. In the obvious confusion someone had made a mistake. I accepted his version and let the matter be.

The contract was signed on 1 December 1989 in a privately hired room at Cardiff Arms Park with Ray Griffiths making all sorts of pronouncements to the media about protecting Welsh Rugby Union players from the mercenary attacks from Rugby League. He was a self-appointed saviour. Not only was he giving a few players a livelihood but also giving them expert advice on fitness, stamina and strength. The press reaction was astonishing.

Here at last, argued some writers in their columns, was the way to protect the game. Welsh players had been leaving the Union game in droves to seek richer pastures in Widnes and Warrington. There was genuine anger that the game and its players could be so vulnerable to the wave of a cheque book. Yet, they were quite prepared to see financial inducements protecting the amateur ethos.

Others, in fact the majority, saw the Griffiths move as a threat to the amateur laws governing the game. Wasn't Mr Griffiths to all intents and purposes paying players in defiance of the laws? There was a fair amount of cynicism flying around, yet I took no heed, since I could rationalise without fear of contradiction that the Xell job was a full-time occupation with an attractive salary. The alternatives were limited. Mark Jones, the Neath no. 8, and Mark Ring of Cardiff were also being courted by Griffiths. Both were out of work, both sought by Rugby League and easy prey for the great London philanthropist.

The venue of the signing, which had all the trappings of a Rugby League or boxing ceremony, was a calculated move. The WRU happened to be staging one of its committee meetings nearby, so with Griffiths rubbing shoulders with Union officers and representatives, suddenly respectability was no problem. He convinced others as he'd convinced me. I signed with his son Damion as a witness. Mark Jones' contract was witnessed by the then coaching organiser, John Dawes. This to him was the Union's stamp of approval, but in truth, John signed the document as a personal favour to Ivor Jones.

I was introduced to Norman Strangemore of Data Media Corporation, who supplied Griffiths with computer software. There was a breakfast meeting held at the Post House Hotel in Cardiff which was attended by Mark Jones, who had also by then signed as an Xell employee, Norman Strangemore, Ray Griffiths and me. Again, it was a session of name-dropping, impressive plans and grandiose ideas. You could not help getting excited. I don't know if he paid the bill for that breakfast, but suddenly we stopped using Post House hotels.

"The usual," he told a waiter at a grand function held at London's Café Royal. Without questioning, the wine waiter returned with champagne. It was a glittering occasion, with celebrities gathered on every table. George Best was there, so too was Welsh international soccer player Jeremy Charles. The Geordie Alan Price supplied the cabaret.

On our way to the Café Royal, Ray Griffiths asked my wife Ann, "What are you going to do with your new-found

37

wealth?" He couldn't resist playing the role of the great Welsh sports benefactor. I noticed that evening how friendly he was with his bank manager. They hardly stopped talking, and seemed to be on good terms. Griffiths could charm financiers and friends as well as rugby players.

Ann and I travelled to Belfast that Christmas to see her folks. Whilst we were there, my mother phoned to tell me that a Dave Harries from Mumbles had called, pretending to invite me to a dinner, but I knew better. He was a Rugby League scout in Wales. He'd left a number for me to ring a Mr Jack Robinson. The telephone code suggested that it was a number in the North of England.

"Perhaps someone is going to make me an offer," I told the family jokingly. Mr Robinson, whoever he might be, wasn't at home, but I managed eventually to make contact. Mr Robinson was chairman of Wigan and they were prepared to offer a fee of £150,000 if I turned professional. He explained that their full-back had become something of a liability and they needed me for a cup match on 9 January. Rugby League had introduced the sixth tackle law and they wanted someone to shunt the ball downfield. I wasn't so concerned about that, but the fee did appeal to me. I recall saying somewhat pompously to him that as I had a degree, I was in a slightly different category from others who had travelled north. It was one of those statements that you regret saying. I've had a few of those.

There were other considerations, of course. Not only the exciting prospect of working with Xell, but the Welsh team were due to go to Portugal on a training course, and I didn't want to abandon ship right there and then.

I needed time to think, so I asked Mr Robinson to contact me in Portugal. The Welsh prop, David Young, happened to be my room-mate at the training camp and he told me of Ray Griffiths' plans to take over the commercial side of Cardiff Rugby Club, of which I naturally knew nothing. We also, funnily enough, discussed Rugby League, and Dai without hesitation said he wasn't interested in playing the game. When he returned, he signed for St Helens.

Jack Robinson phoned me in Portugal and asked me if I

would sign as soon as I arrived back in Wales. I didn't give a commitment but spoke to David Harries, the go-between, and explained that I wanted first of all to get into the Welsh side. That was something of a challenge since the media were behind Anthony Clement of Swansea. He was, claimed the scribes, "a better attacking full-back" and the references to my alleged lack of speed appeared with annoying regularity.

The press boys also got wind of the Wigan offer and suddenly Thorburn had been offered £150,000 by Wigan. I denied that approach at the time, and so did Wigan. I knew, however, that I was only a phone call away from financial security.

"What the hell," I decided. "I might as well cash in." I rang Wigan but got little response. They didn't return my call, which has convinced me that I was a temporary target of theirs to plug a gap. In the final analysis, I suppose it was just as well that I didn't go.

It was still January and my monthly salary from Xell was due. A cheque arrived, but there was no reference to a National Insurance contribution. I contacted Griffiths, who responded with an all-too-familiar phrase.

"Don't worry, we'll sort it out at this end."

At the end of February, there was no cheque at all. The first hints of doubt crept into my mind. Perhaps everything was not all right. Ann and I discussed the matter but decided to give him the chance of explaining what was going wrong. Two months passed and still no money. It was all very disturbing, but as yet I wasn't prepared to admit to a colossal mistake.

My next step was to confront Griffiths at the Cardiff office. He immediately produced a cheque book and wrote out a cheque for the full amount. Four days later the cheque bounced, and I was fuming. Ann was pregnant and I didn't want to worry her. Day by day the situation was becoming more menacing. I travelled to London to meet Griffiths. Again, he wrote out a cheque for the full amount, claiming he'd made a mistake. He wrote a letter to the bank asking them for an explanation. All this was done in my presence, so when I travelled back to Wales I was a little happier.

Everything seemed in order when I checked my account's balance at the Hole-in-the-Wall. Yet four days later the bank informed me that the new cheque had not been honoured and would I call to discuss the matter. Naturally, I was very much embarrassed, since people knew me at the local branch. The news would travel fast on the Welsh bush telegraph that I was in serious financial trouble and had been taken for a ride. A few days after my daughter Kelly's birth, I spoke to Griffiths, who claimed he'd sorted everything out. He invited me to Cardiff to have breakfast with him at the Crest Hotel. I was prepared to give him more than a piece of my mind.

When I arrived he was with John Roberts of JR Management, a public relations and marketing firm. I didn't know him at all well and this prevented me from having a real go at Ray Griffiths. This was a pity, because John, an honourable individual, was also a victim of the Griffiths charm and corruption: JR Management eventually had to go into liquidation as a result of non-payments by Xell.

I flew to Ireland with the Welsh team, Griffiths having again given me an assurance that on my return "everything would be sorted out". Strange as it may seem, I still wanted to believe him. Again, I went down to the cashpoint to see if anything had been done: nothing at all, and I was now owed five months' salary. Ann was devastated, and so was I. My father offered to help me out financially and Berwyn Davies, the Neath solicitor, was approached. Articles began appearing in the press about Griffiths, but still no money.

Wales were off on a summer tour of Namibia, and I honestly didn't know whether I could afford to go. The WRU sent Griffiths a letter asking him whether I would be receiving pay on tour. He didn't have the decency to reply. Fortunately the WRU paid £500 for loss of earnings and the normal daily allowance. It was my only income, and the family needed the money to live on.

When I returned from Namibia, matters got worse. John Roberts, the man I'd met at the breakfast table, phoned me to explain that he was owed £20,000 and hadn't received one penny from Griffiths. The garage where Griffiths had leased cars for Mark Jones and me called to ask when they were going to be paid for. Once again, not a coin had changed hands. John Roberts told me he'd called in the Fraud Squad. I had also spoken to them.

I phoned Griffiths, hoping to shake him into paying me. I spoke to Ivor Jones, who had been present at the initial meetings when we had discussed what Xell could do for me, and what I could do for them. I was dumbstruck. He confessed to not having been paid for three months before I'd signed. Why the hell didn't he warn us? It was a complete and utter shambles. The Fraud Squad paid me another visit and I gave them chapter and verse – the promises, the bounced cheques, the excuses – the lot.

I was told that a number of companies wanted to contact Ray Griffiths. The investigating officers visited Mark Jones and Mark Ring, Cardiff Rugby Club and anyone else with the remotest connection with the man who had made so many promises. I was later to sign a sworn statement as to my involvement with Xell and its owner and the Fraud Squad have kept me informed on developments. It has hardly been a shock to discover that I was not the only one caught.

My financial situation was dire. I was broke and totally devastated. The families gathered around and helped out and the bank offered overdraft facilities. The scale of my financial predicament was more severe than I had thought. The Neath club offered to help, and eventually I accepted a £2,000 loan from the club.

Throughout this period I kept wondering about the vast amount of publicity Griffiths had generated for this company. The only compliment I can pay the man is that he'd had the gall to confront all those people with his amazing fabrication.

The HTV current affairs programme *Wales This Week* asked me to appear on a programme which was investigating the whole affair. Needless to say, they had some difficulty in contacting Griffiths. There was one doorstep interview at Griffiths' home when a woman claiming to be his sister answered the door. Watching the programme I knew full well that the woman was Una, Ray Griffiths' wife.

After the programme I was contacted by a man who said

he'd known Griffiths for twelve years and had loaned him his house for a short duration. It was the house seen in the television programme. He then told me he'd been unable to get Griffiths out of the house, and my former employer had been building extensions at the rear of the house without telling him. Was there no end to this tale? It gave me no pleasure at the time; I was so broke. It was the Griffiths promises that had kept me from signing for Rugby League, and it was the broken promises which gave me no alternative but to gratefully accept the tour allowance when Wales were in Namibia.

It was an amazing web that finally trapped him. On 14 January 1992 Griffiths pleaded guilty to three charges, which included two counts of fraudulent trading and one count of obtaining services by deception. Seven other charges were ordered to 'lie on the file'.

Fortunately, since then my faith in employers has been restored. The offer of employment from Westdale Press was most welcome, and though I knew little about the publishing industry I was grateful to the Cardiff company for the opportunity. Again it meant travelling and selling, but at least I was now dealing with people who were trustworthy.

Eventually I was given an opportunity of working for the Welsh Development Agency. The job entails attracting European and Overseas companies to West Wales: a kind of ambassador, if you like for an area which has been so much a part of me. Perhaps, after all, there will now be some continuity and satisfaction.

4

"Scum of the Earth" and Other Regrettable Sayings

I had left the answerphone on, since I had no desire to talk to anyone. When I eventually played it back there were the usual bleeps of those who had tried unsuccessfully to contact me but had grown weary of waiting. Then came the message I had been dreading.

"Why did you do it? You've brought disgrace to the family and we all feel very ashamed." It was my mother, in tears, reacting to events after the Wales–England match when I waved a rude two-fingered salute to the television cameras and called Stephen Jones of *The Sunday Times* "scum of the earth".

Yes, there are times when you wish the clock could be turned back, and the week after the Arms Park incidents was the worst period of my life. My family couldn't understand why I had done such a thing, nor could Ann, and the players couldn't believe what I had said. I regret what I did immediately after the match, and I regret to this day naming Stephen Jones and have apologised to him, but something was going to happen that weekend because the pressure had been so intense in the build-up to the match.

You couldn't turn on the television or open a newspaper without a former Welsh international being interviewed about England's dismal record at Cardiff. They had gone twenty-six years without winning on Welsh soil. The black and white pictures of the last victory in 1963 appeared with the regularity of the Nine O'Clock News. Pundits, experts, ex-internationals all voiced their opinion that the so-called

43

impregnable walls of Cardiff would come tumbling down. J. P. R. Williams, who had never lost to England at Cardiff, gave his opinion, so did Clive Rowlands as the last losing captain at Cardiff, and on and on they went. It drove me mad as a captain and by match day I was in a tizz.

It wasn't just a match, it was a question of survival. It was desperately close, and Robert Jones played the tactical game of his life with high box kicks. We won by the narrowest of margins. The relief was such that I acted in an impromptu and foolish manner. I was angry because I felt the team had been let down by those who should have known better.

I turned to the cameras and gave the now infamous two-fingered salute. It wasn't directed at the crowd, as some thought. It was meant for all the so-called pundits, the owners of glib rent-a-quote tongues. Some of the reporters, presenters and commentators who had never played a game of rugby in their lives, let alone under any kind of pressure, had had their pulpit moments of opinionated and pious lyricism. It was now my turn, albeit in a more demonstrative manner. Phil Davies did the same, but the cameras didn't catch his gesture. Since the press box is on the other side of Cardiff Arms Park, the press hadn't seen the incident. There followed a press conference and not one question was asked about my action. As usual I met the family after the game but I was still seething with anger. The family knew that something was afoot, since I wasn't myself at all.

Again, what happened at the after-match dinner has been well recorded. Stephen Jones of *The Sunday Times* had argued in his column the previous week that it would do Welsh rugby a power of good if Wales lost to England: at least it would force the Welsh Rugby Union into some kind of positive action. I couldn't believe that a writer, and a Welshman, could ever propose such an illogical argument. Were we supposed to throw the match for the sake of developing the game in Wales? His comments had been gnawing away at me for a week.

I never prepare speeches in minute detail. There are just a few points to make and people to thank. Short and snappy has always been my approach; in other words avoid tedium. That evening I had scribbled down the sentence that was to make headlines.

"I would very much appreciate it if Stephen Jones would leave the room, because I consider people like him to be the scum of the earth."

There wasn't a sharp intake of breath. In fact, I don't recall any response at all. The players couldn't believe their ears, and shortly after the dinner Brian Moore, the England hooker, came over and told me that he wished he, at times, had not held back in telling a few home truths.

The Welsh chairman of selectors, the late Rod Morgan, also had a quiet word. "I'll back you all the way," he said. It sounded like the proverbial vote of confidence from the soccer club chairman before the manager is sacked. I should have known it would snowball into a row, and it did. Instead of becoming a celebration of a win over England it became Thorburn's notorious weekend. The rest of the evening was spent with Ann and the Welsh party. Ann couldn't believe I had been so foolish and I suppose we had something of a row.

I do regret having singled out Stephen Jones, especially when I found he'd given me such a complimentary report the next morning. The anger was within me, an uncontrollable desire to hit back, and once the pressure of the game was over my emotions got the better of me.

The other regret is hurting my family, who have always been so supportive. On Sunday, I met my brothers at Gowerton; I told them what had happened. They were mortified. I explained the reasons behind my comments and I suppose they were accepted with dubious enthusiasm. John Billot of the *Western Mail* had already been in touch to ask whether I meant to say what I did. At that time in the heat of the moment I told him that I was sticking to every word.

On the Sunday evening I phoned Stephen Jones to apologise. His wife answered the phone and I explained who I was. "Oh," came the reply and Stephen came to the phone. I said I was sorry that I had singled him out and that it had been wrong of me. He was extremely understanding and explained that he didn't realise that what he wrote in his paper had such an effect on players. We finished our conversation on friendly terms.

Blissfully unaware of what had happened, my father left for London full of enthusiasm about the Welsh win. The Sunday press had not picked up the two-fingered salute yet. So when the jubilant Mr Thorburn went to work on Monday he was greeted with the back page headlines and the unspoken censure of colleagues.

The following week was sheer hell. My stomach churned as the bulletins once again repeated the incident. There was little said about the game, only the action of the captain who had disgraced the Welsh jersey. The depression went deeper.

If I had been in contention for a Lions tour I had now blown it. I was never invited to play for the Barbarians again. Yet of the twenty or so letters I received after the weekend only one was abusive. It was from an English fan who thought my gesture had been directed towards the England fans. Nothing could be further from the truth. My target was far more dangerous – Welsh know-it-alls.

Stephen Jones' comment that he didn't know that players were affected by what he wrote doesn't carry much weight with me. If what the journalists write is of no importance, why do they bother writing it in the first place? They are meant to be professional writers, paid by their newspapers so that people can read their thoughts and analysis. So many of them have no deep understanding of what they are writing about. I am prepared to listen to reasonable comment, but utterances from people in highly paid jobs who have no knowledge of or feeling for the game deserve the cold shoulder. On the other hand, criticisms from ex-international players, some of them contemporaries of mine, are particularly cutting and hard to swallow. They, more than anyone, should know the pressures of the international arena, yet some of their comments are the harshest. How did they react when the press columns were so critical that they couldn't bear to read them? Perhaps they need to justify their existence, perhaps they feel that they were superior. Perhaps they have forgotten what it was like; again, perhaps it's easier to be outstanding in a successful side. I watched these players as a schoolboy with fond admiration. No longer do I feel that some of them deserve that adulation. Imagine what I felt on entering the Welsh changing room in Paris for the first time to find myself sharing those anxious moments in the company of giants like Gareth Davies and Terry Holmes. Then imagine how I felt when Terry in particular gave me a hard time in his column, repeating the "non-attacking full-back" clap-trap. It didn't make sense then, and it still doesn't. If it's difficult to accept criticism from your peers, it's nigh impossible to entertain comments from people who have never played the game seriously.

I can recall Bob Symonds of HTV at the end of a televised provincial game in New Zealand making one absolutely outrageous observation. Grant Fox, wearing a head bandage, had been kicking conversions and penalties from everywhere. At the end of the highlights Symonds turned to the camera and said, "If Wales had a kicker of his standard we'd let him wear a nappy on his head." This from an ITV commentator, and a *Welshman* to boot! We all make statements which we afterwards regret. I had by that time broken the Welsh and Neath club records for points gathering.

Reams and reams of opinionated articles arrive on the country's doorsteps every morning from people with varying qualifications to pass judgement. A match report is one thing, but the interpretation at times is bewildering. Perhaps it is an ego trip for some of them; perhaps others are forced by their editors into making value judgements. How many of them have ever considered how the indi-vidual or the subject of their character assassination would react? Being an "outspoken" critic is a burden for some. They mistake fact and fiction too often.

In Wales it is particularly galling. Rugby is followed, no matter how the national team is doing, with intense fervour. Rugby dominates the back pages of newspapers every morning, even during the cricket season. The players from England, Scotland and Ireland have no idea how taxing this becomes. I think it would be fair to say that papers in other parts of the UK only give priority to rugby coverage during the Five Nations Championship or when Will Carling's team decide not to speak to the press pack. In Wales the coverage is morning, noon and night, every reporter looking for a different angle, quote or story. I confess that I have no regard for some of them, because I suspect that they haven't a clue about the game or any love for it, which is the greater sin.

If all this sounds bitter, it is probably because I have taken more than my fair share of criticism. No one knows better than the individual player if he has performed below par, but it would benefit some of these fresh-faced experts, especially in the Welsh papers and radio, if they bore in mind that no player intentionally goes on to the field to play badly.

My father used to admire John Reason of the *Sunday Telegraph* but after he suggested that a sundial moved faster than I did, Dad decided that Steve Bale was a more constructive commentator. And then there is Mr Wooller – he of rugby, cricket and outrageous comment fame. I do not know the man but have heard many a tale about his observations about humanity, industry, religion, the Welsh language, and anything else under the sun. When Noel Mannion scored his famous try for Ireland at Cardiff, running away after Bleddyn Bowen's kick had been charged down, Wooller wanted to know where I had been. Noel ran for the line almost unchallenged and Mr Wooller wrote, "And where was Thorburn, I ask myself?"

Now, here lies the dilemma: it is one thing to be caught out of position, it is another to be castigated by the press for not being enough of an attacking full-back. It seems impossible to satisfy the Welsh press, since their primary motive seems to be to influence the selection of the national side, but then accept no responsibility for the consequences.

As the television pictures showed, I had been alongside Bleddyn waiting for what could have been a try-scoring pass. Unfortunately Bleddyn kicked, Noel caught the ball and the entire Welsh team was caught flat-footed.

I was incensed by Wooller's comments and phoned to ask him if he fully realised what had been going on. Since so much had been written about my lack of attacking play, had he appreciated the significance of any move down the left wing?

He was unimpressed. "In my day the last line of defence was the full-back," he replied, and proceeded to offer me advice on how to play the position. We parted company on the phone unable to agree on anything.

The tale does not end there, however. My mother had also seen the article and was equally angered by the injustice of the comment. She wrote a polite letter to Wilf Wooller under her maiden name, enclosing a pair of spectacles to aid his all-round vision.

"Dear Miss Jenkins," came the reply from the Wooller household, "My wife is an ophthalmic optician, and she assures me that there is nothing wrong with my eyesight and so I have deposited the glasses in the bin." I think that both parties were satisfied with the correspondence. It was not the only letter that my mother wrote in my defence. I know of some, but I suspect there were many others.

The chairman of the Welsh selectors, the late Rod Morgan, also received a caustic letter when I had been dropped by Wales. This time my mother used the address of my great-aunt, who turned up at our house one day, slightly puzzled at having received a "very nice letter from a certain Mr Morgan" whom she didn't know at all, but did we think that she was being considered? The Welsh team must be desperate!

Indeed, it's difficult to assess how great an influence the media wields in rugby circles. I prefer to think that the selectors know what they are doing and are unaffected by what is written; yet I suspect that there are times when repetition or even locally inspired press campaigns have won the day.

At Neath, Brian Thomas saw to it that press articles were pinned to the changing room wall. There is no better motivator than a bad, uninformed press cutting.

Whereas Cardiff, Newport and Swansea have their "Home" journalists, Neath doesn't have a widely read newspaper, nor can it boast an ex-player turned writer who commands regional or national attention. Steve Bale of the *Independent* is a Neath man, and doesn't begrudge our success as a team, whereas others seem to do so. Unfortunately, he is at the Gnoll far too little. There is no suggestion on my part of advocating favourable or loaded articles – only a fair assessment of what the journalist witnesses, rather than what he wants to see.

Is it mere coincidence that Cardiff receive more than adequate coverage even during indifferent seasons when the entire Cardiff press entourage is present at the Arms Park? It's a formidable team with Barry John *(Daily Express)*, Bleddyn Williams *(Sunday People)*, Wilf Wooller *(Sunday Telegraph)*, and Gerald Davies *(The Times)* formulating attitudes at breakfast tables. I would be the last to accuse them of intentional bias, but I know how I feel about Neath, and I assume that they are just as dedicated. It's a joke among players outside the Cardiff circle that if you want good press, there is nothing better than a lunchtime pint at Cardiff Athletic Club.

For these reasons, I don't think Neath has been given a fair hearing. Success has come from virtually nothing and our domination of the Welsh club scene in recent years has never been fully acknowledged by the Welsh press. True, they report our scores and winning campaigns, but there is an undercurrent of resentment which has been difficult to ignore.

Neath kept winning towards the late 80s and the early 90s, but constant reference was made to Swansea's magical threequarters or the running skills of Llanelli's backs. I don't deny them their talents, but I believe that at Neath we had the finest unit in the country, equal to any and better than most. It all came to a crunch as far as Neath was concerned when Barry John in his *Daily Express* column told the world that the Cardiff pack would take Neath apart in a vital league match. He, like Gerald, is a "Cardiff" journalist, and the column had done the rounds at the Gnoll changing room.

Suffice it to say that the boys in black tore the blue-and-blacks apart. After the match the television cameras were allowed into the changing room to be greeted by chants of "Barry John, Barry John". I confess that I didn't join in, because I had by then learnt my lesson.

However, when Gerald Davies wrote his piece in *The Times* about our close-shaven heads, I did engineer the response. We were due to play Bridgend in the Cup Final, and preparations were made to have a good time at the final whistle, whatever the result. Gerald's comments would not be forgotten, and they offered us a glorious opportunity of a little theatrical one-upmanship. The Yellow Pages were thumbed for a joke or a stage shop in the Swansea and Neath area, and eventually I found what I wanted. The entire Neath squad was kitted out with long-haired wigs, and it was agreed that should we win the Cup every one of us would parade in front of the cameras complete with shaggy-dog hairdos.

The game won, we chickened out, since it would probably have provided another opportunity to have a go at us. Later, though, at the official reception at the WRU Centenary Suite, we did put the wigs on. The effect was astonishing, laughable and intentionally outrageous. It was too much for one supporter.

"You boys are disgusting," he said. "It's disgraceful that you should take the mickey out of Welsh rugby."

The referee, Clive Norling, intervened and from his height turned on the fan.

"Hey listen," he said. "You've been invited to this function: either shut your trap or get out." Good on you, Clive, because the whole matter was done in jest, with perhaps a little rebuke for Gerald.

At one stage, I was determined not to be lured into the media. It would, I told myself, be entirely hypocritical to join a group for which I had scant respect. During the Australian tour, a Welsh rugby journalist admitted in a relaxed moment that he knew very little about the game; we had long suspected as much.

After I retired, a few offers came from London and regional newspapers asking for opinions and comment especially during the World Cup. I had no reservations about radio and television interviews, since – perhaps somewhat innocently – I thought the editors couldn't

51

change what had been recorded. I have since been educated in the techniques of dramatic editing cuts and out-of-context reportage.

The written media were different. I had been misquoted often enough, but when the *Western Mail* asked me for a weekly column, which would not be altered, it seemed a welcome opportunity.

My retirement story was sold to the *People*. I was warned often enough that it would be written in such a way as to cause maximum effect. They are in the business of selling newspapers, which is far removed from the depressions of a Welsh full-back. Such was my frustration at that point, that a statement was prepared for me which was accurate and truthful. Too much so, because after a sleepless night, I decided that the language was too strong and in all probability would reflect on certain individuals.

The original statement had already been sent to the *People* and their rugby writer Terry Godwin. Naturally, they were enthusiastic about my comments, since the temperature was probably right and wouldn't have required many adjustments. On reflection, though I was determined to tell the truth, I felt the language was a bit strong. Much to their disappointment, I toned down the article, but to see it on the Sunday morning with an "I QUIT" headline and the supplementary statements, gave me another lesson in media relations. Tamper with them at your peril!

I assume that the occasional offer will still be made. If it is, I will endeavour both to say exactly what I feel and to be constructive. The column in the *Western Mail* has apparently already angered some of the journalists, since they feel that writing about the game is their prerogative and certainly not to be trivialised by ex-international players.

If I succeed in giving people an insight into what goes on, bearing in mind that few of the current writers have any idea about contemporary pressures, then I shall feel justified in doing so. At present, I am probably too close to the game, with a point or two to prove with Neath. As with my rugby career, I find myself having to convince people. If sincerity in getting a message through counts for something, I shall have little discomfort in writing alongside the word merchants.

5

Helicopters, Resignations, QCs and the Inland Revenue

I am no politician, and "economy with the truth" doesn't come easily to me. I have done things which I have regretted and have accepted the consequences. If you are surrounded by hypocrisy, which is often the case in the circles that I have been associated with, then it is difficult to remain afloat, let alone aloof.

If, as Gerald Davies once wrote of me in *The Times*, "There remains only reluctant approval; praise is only grudgingly given", I will stand my corner with or without outside support. Others may hide behind half-truths and innuendos or, as the late John Kendall-Carpenter, secretary of the International Rugby Board, once said, "in that great, seething Welsh pot-pourri, that always unsavoury goulash of a dark and dirty Celtic colour and smell". I could never attempt to be so lyrical, but I think I know what he means. Perhaps it is best known as deviousness. I think it was David Watkins, the former Welsh outside-half, who once said that after being dropped by his country he found himself confronted individually by five selectors who all confided in him that they had voted for his inclusion. *C'est la vie*.

The Lions had won their '89 Test series in Australia and I was captain of the Wales "B" tour in Canada. I might have been selected for the Lions tour, but for the incidents after that England game. It was no use regretting the foolish act of an emotional moment, but a Lions tour had been an ambition ever since I established myself in the Welsh team. It remains a hope that I might still be good enough for consideration next year despite being out of the inter-national spotlight. Yet during our Canadian tour through the Rockies I was asked by the Welsh team manager, Denzil Lloyd, if I had been invited to South Africa for that country's centenary celebrations. Denzil has his own special way of asking questions: you are not quite sure whether the answer is more important than the question.

The rugby press columns had been full of speculation about a World XV being invited to play against the Springboks during their centenary celebrations. I told Denzil, ironically later to become a member of the Inter-national Rugby Board, that I had received no such invitation.

On my return from Canada the invitation was waiting for me at home. A letter had been sent, signed by Alex Kellerman of the South African Rugby Board, and it was accompanied by a letter from the WRU signed by the then President, Clive Rowlands, and secretary, David East. It said that the Welsh Rugby Union was obliged to pass on the invitation. There was no suggestion that we should decline, it was a simple exercise in passing on a message.

It was the beginning of a bitter saga which resulted in the resignations of the WRU secretary, the sacking of the two Welsh representatives on the IRB, an inquiry led by a QC, the resignation and subsequent reinstatement of Clive Rowlands as the WRU President, and a military under-cover operation which would have done the SAS proud. As players we were rudderless, since the administration apparently condemned the tour but acted as messengers. Certain senior members of the executive paid lip service to the Union's official declared policy, and, as shall be seen later, a number of executives quietly packed their bags.

It was some sight, I can tell you, when the Welsh Rugby Union was officially welcomed, to find eight representatives on South African soil, when the Union had been instructed by its member clubs to sever links.

I was called the chief recruiter of the Welsh players, or the *agent provocateur* in the report published by Vernon Pugh, QC. His full report was intended to be confidential and only an abridged version was sent to the member clubs.

As to the full statements, the world was told that the evidence had been shredded. Copies must have been available, or miraculously committed to memory, since I heard passages quoted liberally in bars and on touchlines. The shredder must have been missing a tooth or two.

The abbreviated report was also meant to be confidential but the press got hold of it before the member clubs of the Union. Ah well! That is Wales, a village from end to end, where newspapers unsuccessfully vie with the bush telegraph to spread the word. I cannot deny that in the final stages I was co-ordinator of the transport arrangements to London for the invited players from Wales, but a week earlier, of the ten who eventually travelled I only knew of five who had definitely been invited. The remainder of the party were recruited by others, who have yet to be identified. Names have been mentioned, but only speculative evidence produced. The accusatory nod, though, is severe enough for the people concerned. There seems little point in pleading innocence in Wales once you've been "named".

The normal conversation with some of the fans is an educating experience.

"You're Paul Thorburn, aren't you? You were the one who organised that South African tour, weren't you? I know it's you 'cause it was in the papers, see. There you are, Idwal, I told you it was him. I saw it in the *Post*".

No use pleading innocence. Might as well get on with the custodial sentence.

On the original letter which I received it mentioned the names of other Welsh players who had been asked to attend the centenary celebrations: Mike Hall and Robert Norster of Cardiff, Robert Jones and Anthony Clement of Swansea, all returning Lions from Australia were on that list, and myself.

The first reaction was one of delight, since I had always had an ambition of travelling to play in South Africa. So many ex-internationals talked in awe of their experiences both on and off the field, and here was a country which wanted to compete with the best in the world. I was aware of the WRU member clubs' decision to discontinue all links, and I was continually being made aware of the huge

56

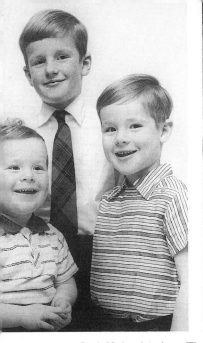

ABOVE LEFT: *Paul, Neil and Andrew. The player, the brain and the tour operator*

ABOVE RIGHT: *An early practice session*   BELOW: *The Thorburn clan for Dad's 60th*

OPPOSITE TOP LEFT: *First the Palace. Then fish and chips on the way home*

OPPOSITE TOP RIGHT: *Got there at last! University College, Swansea*

OPPOSITE BELOW LEFT: *Mr and Mrs*

OPPOSITE BELOW RIGHT: *That's a long way, Dad!*

TOP: *Captain of Hereford Cathedral School U-13s*

BELOW: *Fourteen years later at Murrayfield*

ABOVE LEFT: *Not just a kicker*

ABOVE RIGHT: *Jonathan Davies – overlooked by Llanelli, nurtured by Neath, bought by Widnes*

BELOW: *Manchester United look out! L to R: Dai Morgan, Alan Edmunds, Jeremy Pugh, Glen Webbe, David Bishop, Paul Thorburn, Phil Pugh, Jonathan Davies, Steve Powell, Phil Bennett, Leighton Phillips, Barry John, Elgan Rees, Rowland Phillips*

OPPOSITE TOP LEFT: *A black day for us. Neath v New Zealand*

OPPOSITE TOP RIGHT: *Brian and Kevin – sired and sheared in Welsh West Wales*

OPPOSITE BELOW: *Heineken League Champions 1990/91*

ABOVE: *The two faces of Ron Waldron: success with Neath, strain with Wales*

BELOW LEFT: *Brian Thomas – "Don't call me Ayatollah!"*

BELOW RIGHT: *The new Welsh man Robert Norster getting his point over!*

OPPOSITE TOP LEFT: *David Campese: 1991 was Campo's World Cup*

OPPOSITE TOP RIGHT: *Serge Blanco, a record and shoulder breaker*

OPPOSITE BELOW: *Phillipe Sella, a world-class playmaker*

ABOVE: *Stephen Jones of the* Sunday Times *– I rang to apologise*

RIGHT: *The late John Kendall Carpenter – he gave us the all clear on South Africa*

BELOW: *Shaking hands with Ray Griffiths, Xell. The early days*

protest in South Wales against the apartheid system. I have no hesitation in condemning the system. It is unfair, and the sooner legislation is completed to totally dismantle it, the better. However, it has relatively little to do with playing rugby. If all the injustices in the world were brought into play as a tool against sporting links, the world would be a sorry place indeed.

The prominent members of the Anti-Apartheid movement continue to protest that as rugby players we do not see the real South Africa even when visiting there. They have a point. I've hardly seen anything of any other country I've visited apart from viewing the outside world from inside a bus. There's little time between training sessions and games. I wonder how many of the rugby tourists to our country have enough time to see the "real" Wales, England, Scotland and Northern Ireland. I am also convinced that the same questions are never asked of other travellers, businessmen, holiday tourists and academics. So why should sportsmen be singled out as the world's observers of social injustice and racial inequality? That is the brief of politicians and not of try-scorers, run-getters and strikers.

Nothing would stop me from going there. It was a grand opportunity, and the fact that there were real signs that the system was being dismantled gave the South African rugby authorities enough incentive to pursue their objective of establishing first-class international rugby there again.

I began phoning the other lads on the invited list to discuss what we were going to do. Already the papers were full of speculation, with half the England team being named as confirmed tourists and a healthy contribution from Australia and France. However, Rob Norster had conducted his own survey and the picture was a little confusing. Though he had been approached during the Lions tour, the guarantee that the team would be a strong gathering of Australian, French and Lions, was being constantly undermined. The South Africans, it appeared, had misread the situation and were being given little co-operation from their fellow members on the International Board.

This was not much of a surprise to them, and the response from some quarters, especially Transvaal, was to organise a wholly professional tour, thus flouting the authority of the IRB and John Kendall-Carpenter. Those players who had been quoted as saying they would travel were now hesitant, since the penalties for being part of an *ad hoc* travelling circus after the experience of the New Zealand Cavaliers would be severe.

Two things happened which resulted in an amazing volte-face. Threatened by a bizarre professional tour of players who had seen greener days and by possible expulsion from the world of international rugby, the South African Rugby Board sent two representatives to the UK to recruit a legitimate team. John Kendall-Carpenter also gave his blessing to the tour and was to act as mediator and messenger on behalf of the IRB, or so we were allowed to believe. The tour at this point was in danger of collapsing.

The Welsh players decided, for a variety of reasons, not to go. We didn't know the composition of the team and we knew that if we committed ourselves to going, there would be a major political storm. A number of the grounds and training facilities in Wales are owned by Labour-controlled local councils and there was little doubt that if players from certain clubs were to declare their intention of supporting the tour, the recriminations would be felt by their clubs. It wasn't worth the hassle. Whereas rugby players in London can hide behind the anonymity of the big city, we knew that we would have phone calls at any hour of the day and doorstepping television crews, as well as repeated daily question-and-answer sessions in the local shops. The rugby player in Wales is public property. Moreover, John Ryan, the Welsh coach was reported as saying that no player going on the tour would be considered for the Welsh Squad. Bob Norster remained quiet but I said on television that I had made up my mind to refuse the invitation.

A week later Paul Rendall, the England prop, phoned to tell me that he had been approached and that both he and Jeff Probyn had decided to go. Their contact had been Cobus Kotzee, a representative of the South African Rugby Board who was in the country hoping to persuade players to accept the invitations. It wasn't long before he made contact and began listing the likely squad party. Apart from the England players, he told me that Sella, Charvet, Mesnel and Cecillon of France had given assurances as well as a number of the Australians. Willie John McBride had accepted an invitation to manage the team, and his fellow Ballymena clubman Steve Smith, in defiance of the Irish Rugby Board, had also decided to go. There was news from Australia, too, that a small contingent had accepted invitations. With only a couple of weeks to go it seemed that the SARB in conjunction with their First National Bank sponsors would realise their dream.

I still had doubts, having been caught out so often after accepting invitations on assurances made that so-and-so would be there, only to find promises not kept and the eventual teams a pale shadow of those advertised. The Barbarians are famous for this, especially on their Easter tour of Wales. However, Cobus was a convincing salesman.

I decided to have a meeting at home of the players in Wales who had received invitations. Robert Jones turned up and Paul Turner of Newport phoned to tell me he'd be coming too, since he'd been approached by another go-between. Until that phone call I didn't know that Paul had been contacted and to this day I don't know, nor have I asked, who approached him.

There was a meeting the following weekend in London attended by the English internationals, the tour manager Willie John McBride, and Steve Smith from Ireland, Cobus Kotzee and a Sports Marketing agent from South Africa and another SARB representative, Bob Norster and myself. Crucially, the meeting was also attended by John Kendall-Carpenter of the International Rugby Board to give the tour official backing.

Again assurances were given that the touring party would be strong enough to meet the challenges of the Springboks, who had taken to a monastic rugby existence and were just dying to have a go at international opposition.

The biggest surprise of that meeting was the reading of the touring party list. Apart from the original players on the letter written by Alex Kellerman and sent in a WRU envelope, to my utter astonishment there were five other Welshmen on it!

Paul Turner of Newbridge I knew about, but by this time David Pickering, Phil Davies, Mark Ring and Phil John of Pontypridd had been added. Everyone named had been mentioned as possible tour candidates in the Welsh rugby press, which on this occasion seemed to be better informed than anyone in the Union or elsewhere. Someone had been doing a remarkable recruiting and leaking job and though much was written to the effect that the former chairman of Newport, Brian Jones, and the Pontypool solicitor, Terry Vaux, were involved, apart from one phone call from Brian Jones, I had no dealings with them. He phoned me to establish whether I had accepted the invitation.

At that London meeting Bob and I decided to accept. The argument had already been voiced by the Australian contingent that we should be compensated for time lost from work and the inevitable hostility towards us from certain quarters. It was also accepted that this was a tour not recognised by some, though secretly blessed by many on the Four Home Unions Committee; therefore, the normal restrictions should not apply. Our wives and girl-friends would accompany us. The arguments were not new to the South Africans, and the compensation clauses and other requests were accepted.

The promises were kept and the tour was on. There would also be a tour kit and, of course, the opportunity of playing what the SARB representatives regarded to be the world's best. We also knew that the very mention of new kit would persuade Phil Davies to go; he has always had a thing about smart kit, and the mere hint of a tracksuit or leisure wear sends him into raptures.

There was sufficient incentive for both Bob and me to change our minds. The sceptics were to have a field day, with accusations from one end of the country to the other that we had been paid to change our minds, that small fortunes had changed hands, that Swiss and Luxembourg accounts had been opened. We were accused of betraying the game and our nation and of being mercenary. I can categorically state that I, and the others involved, only made sure that we didn't lose out, nor would our families or employers. There was, much later of course, the setting up of an Inland Revenue investigation into allegations of illegal payments, as well as the Welsh Rugby Union cross-examination. Neither the well-informed press, nor the Vernon Pugh WRU inquiry, nor the Inland Revenue have brought any accusations or charges into the public domain. The only charge against the players was that there were inconsistencies in our replies, together with a statement that the panel thought our evidence had been well rehearsed.

It really is laughable. For anyone sitting in a court, listening to police spokesmen giving evidence, there is a massive gap between the prosecution evidence and that of the defence. It is part and parcel of our legal system. As to having rehearsed our replies, I still don't know how some of the players were invited. All this we had to endure as rugby players pursuing a sport we enjoy.

I have mentioned the compensation for lost work, which I believe should be the norm for any player involved in a long tour. Apart from any other consideration I am not political and never will be; I detest politics. To me, it was now a simple matter that we were going to be well looked after and both Ann and I were going to South Africa on what was after all a rugby holiday.

If I had been paid the alleged massive sums of money in order to change my mind – £50,000 was I believe the highest figure quoted – I doubt whether I would have had to go cap in hand to my parents for a loan when the Xell job fell through a few months after returning home. Having my club Neath fork out an interest-free loan because of my financial predicament during my bouncing-cheque period with Xell doesn't sound like a man who has received a tax-free South African bonanza. I don't gamble, either.

The expenses were good, but in a matter of weeks after returning home, I had all the worries of a young family with weekly bills and a red current account. The hotels were excellent and the fact that our wives were invited along was a bonus. My mind was made up. The tour had official IRB

61

backing. It was a good deal, but I knew there would be problems. I didn't envisage the complete collapse of the WRU Politburo, nor the recriminations that were to come. I had enough problems: I was broke, and my employer wasn't providing any monthly cheque.

When we had mentioned to the London meeting the likely opposition to our presence in South Africa, little did we know that the repercussions would be so damaging. It would take a politician to foresee such things, and politicians we were certainly not.

The Welsh playing contingent had problems, however. Whereas Willie John and the England members were winging their way to South Africa, the WRU and its coach, John Ryan, had called for a long weekend squad training session at Aberystwyth. It was made abundantly clear that if we missed that session, it would be curtains on any future international ambitions. So we had a problem. Not only that, but Robert Jones and Anthony Clement were still sticking to their guns and were adamant that they would not be travelling. Tony, especially, was reluctant since his firm had several contracts with Labour-controlled councils in South Wales, and he was sure he would lose his job if he went.

Time was short and I took it upon myself to act as a travel agent, but not as a recruiter of players. Much later in the subsequent WRU inquiry report I was to be called the "principal liaison man who readily agreed to contact other Welsh players and did so". As the current captain of the team that was a natural administrative role for me to accept. Those who I knew had received invitations did make contact, and I was in touch with them, but to call me the principal liaison man is stretching even legal licence a bit far. The initial invitation had been sent to five players. I have no idea who contacted the other five. I certainly didn't. As it was, my phone bill was colossal.

The Welsh squad training camp was at Aberystwyth, not the most accessible of places, and it was scheduled to run from Thursday until Sunday morning. I knew that in order to get the South African flight from Heathrow on the Sunday night, we would have to leave Aberystwyth early on Sunday. The Lions players who had returned from Australia were allowed to go home on Saturday, so it wouldn't be a logistical problem for them. For the rest of us, without giving the game away, the late departure from Mid-Wales called for drastic measures. The South African agents were made aware of our dilemma. I'll say this for them, if anything comes between them and their rugby, there are few problems which cannot be solved. This was a mere nuisance factor to be resolved with a few phone calls.

The Welsh exit was going to be a "task force" operation. We knew that the press and the protesters would expect us to leave by car and head for London once the training had finished. The wives had already organised themselves with hired taxis to take them to Heathrow in order to meet us. They also had our luggage with them. Ann had to make special arrangements, since she was in Belfast. The Lions who had left Aberystwyth on the Saturday would be waiting at Cardiff Airport for a helicopter ride to London. Whatever else this South African tour would turn out to be, it was never going to be ordinary.

Cobus thought it unwise to ask the helicopters to land at Aberystwyth, so an alternative landing venue had to be arranged. We contacted Aberaeron Rugby Club, a few miles down the Cardigan Bay coastline, and asked permission to land on their field. They were more than willing to help out.

On the Friday night, the Welsh squad had a night out in an Aberystwyth pub. It was here, after some persuasive chat, that Robert Jones and Anthony Clement changed their minds. As the beers went by, Robert said he would join us, and immediately phoned his wife Megan to pack the bags and join the rest of the wives. Anthony went through the same operation. Robert tried to get in touch with his father-in-law, Clive Rowlands, knowing what the implications might be for the President of the Welsh Rugby Union, but Clive could not be contacted. This was extremely unfortunate, since Clive arrived in Aberystwyth the following morning to be told by the Welsh coach, John Ryan, that Robert and Megan had left for South Africa. He was livid, since it placed him in the unenviable and delicate position of defending the Union stand against links with South Africa, while knowing full well that members of his family were on a Johannesburg-bound flight. It was the beginning of what was to become a most damaging episode in Welsh rugby history. It was also one of the most hypocritical.

With the presence of the International Board secretary at crucial meetings, the players were under the impression that the tour carried with it the support of that august body. Invitations had been passed on to us via the Welsh Rugby Union and later we were to learn that other players had received their invitations via their unions as well.

By Sunday morning there were now eleven players from Wales bound for South Africa. Accusations were soon flying around South Wales that members of the WRU had acted dishonourably, organising every move behind the scenes without permission from the Union secretary, David East. To this day, I do not know who was responsible, but the resignations of Terry Vaux and Gwilym Treharne from the International Rugby Board were sought after our return. R. H. Williams, a selector who denied that he was going to South Africa, only to be filmed at Heathrow before departure, was forced out of office. The blood-letting was to go on for some considerable time. The players would be accused of disobeying the Union party line, when certain senior members of the executive were flouting a policy endorsed by a substantial majority at an extraordinary meeting convened by the Union. To say that the situation was a little confusing was a gross understatement. Meanwhile, the players had a tour to think about.

Once the training camp had broken up, the cars headed out of Aberystwyth, past the dozen or so protesters and the press group, and down the coast road to Aberaeron. The timing had to be right. The helicopters were waiting for us at Aberaeron and we joined the other players and our wives at Heathrow. It was as simple as that. The move was superbly organised by Cobus, with the Welsh press seething with anger, so that we were allowed to exercise our freedom as rugby players, and not as pawns in the hypocritical Welsh rugby political shop window. This time, there had been no one to leak our arrangements.

On arrival in South Africa, we were greeted by our hosts. The rest of the party had already been there a week and had played. Naturally, the tour had attracted huge interest in South Africa, let alone at home – though for different reasons.

My first recollection is of the kitting-out room. The amazing kit, it transpired, didn't impress even Phil Davies. The colour scheme, a lurex blue, was fairly horrible. But the boots. Ah well, now that is a different matter. I'm told the Welsh have gained a reputation when on tour of grabbing everything that is going. Perhaps it's because in the past we've been offered so little. When other unions were negotiating kit deals with leading manufacturers, the WRU was buying off-the-peg tracksuits from Marks and Spencer. We were shown into a room by the South African Adidas reps and offered boots for the tour. I don't know what happened to Phil John, the Pontypridd hooker, but he seemed intent on kitting out his whole club team when he got home. I'm sure he took half a dozen pairs of boots with him, and Mark Ring wasn't so slow in depositing his well-worn trainers and walking out with a brand new pair. I'm sure the Adidas boys have never seen anything like it, but suddenly the Welsh kitbags had become very heavy indeed.

But despite all the grandiose promises, the kit was none too clever: lurid, noticeable and hardly what Phil Davies, our resident expert on sartorial elegance had anticipated. You could see the whole squad many miles away, which I suppose was the intention.

The second disappointment was a domestic one, and until the problem was resolved, after a barrage of protestations, it threatened to spoil the tour. As soon as we arrived the players and their wives were separated and directed to different hotels. Having been promised and enticed by the luxury of an all-expenses-paid rugby holiday, we felt that this was too much. Ann, I know, was extremely angry and made her opinions clear. The other wives were also incensed by this enforced celibate rugby life. It took some time to convince Willie John McBride, our manager, that we were annoyed by this unexpected change to the itinerary – though I suspect that he was enjoying the company of his wife throughout the tour.

So, we used the tactics of our college days. I went to Ann's hotel in the evenings, stayed the night and returned to the team hotel early next morning. It felt just like those charming WRU habits, when a player was not allowed to have his wife or girlfriend near him until the Committee had declared that it was safe to do so. Many a night on post-match weekends, the single beds and bath tubs of Cardiff hotels have creaked under the weight of married couples. That has now changed, but only recently.

Eventually, the South African authorities relented, and normal relations were resumed. However, a certain diplomatic damage had occurred. It did have its lighter moments. At least I can look back at the incident with some mirth now. At the time it was deadly serious. A South African newspaper reporter had noted that the players and wives were living apart and asked my wife Ann what she thought of the situation. Ann has a wicked streak of humour and in jest answered, "Well, the boys might prefer sleeping together!" That was it. The next morning the headlines proclaimed the tourists as "gays" and "queers". Mrs Thorburn was not at all amused; nor for that matter were the other wives.

The team was coached by Bob Templeton, a worldly-wise rugby man from Australia, with painstaking attention to detail and to the opposition's weaknesses. However, it soon became apparent that the real gaffer was the captain, scrum-half and current French coach, Pierre Berbizier. This was bad news for our Robert Jones, because Berbizier, if fit, would play in the test matches.

Our first match as Welsh tourists was a bit of a disaster. Twenty-four hours off the plane, we were confronted by the President's XV, a thinly disguised South African "B" team. Mike Hall cried off, much to the disgust of Denis Charvet, who had to play a second game, and the team composition was predominantly Welsh. This caused a few wry remarks that the Welsh had arrived to weaken the touring team.

It was immediately evident, if we hadn't realised it before, that the South Africans, having been denied international exposure, were going to make up for lost time. To put it bluntly, we were stuffed, despite the valiant efforts of Ian Williams, the Australian wing, with two fine tries. In retrospect, we should not have agreed to play so soon, because many of us were below par. It sounded fine at the time, and we wanted to honour our hosts, but a few reputations were damaged, and the Welsh, apart from Mike Hall and Bob Norster, became the tour's second stringers.

It was also our first look at the South African opposition. As ever, they looked large and mean, yet probably didn't have the finesse of the tourists, who had been exposed to international opposition on a regular basis. After playing against Northern Transvaal as well, we found that provincial rugby was a few degrees stronger than the national XV. This was understandable, since the Currie Cup was everything to the South African rugby player, and the lack of opportunity to play as a unit had left them searching for a style. The politics of South African rugby, we were told, had also become a victim of parochialism: each province was highly suspicious of the others. All this was familiar talk to a Welshman, of course. My regret was knowing that a few games between South Africa and the New Zealanders or Australians would soon settle matters, and the inter-provincial squabbling would soon give way to the national cause; whereas in Wales the inter-club rivalry, with all its damaging effects, would continue well after apartheid had been demolished.

We saw little of the country, and wherever we went, rarely roaming freely, the security was strict. There was one occasion when we were invited to stage a rugby clinic at a black township. On board the bus there were several security officers, armed and tense. At the back of the bus stood a soldier with a large machine gun covered by a cloak. We were left with no illusions as to what would happen if there was trouble. As we approached the town-

67

ship we were told that there had been disturbances ahead, and a plume of smoke could be seen in the distance. The bus slowed down and it attracted attention. The decision was immediately taken to turn around, and our gunman at the back had already uncovered his gun.

A few schoolboys approached, calmly walking back home, but this was enough to convince Bob Norster, one of the most nervous people I've met, that we were about to be attacked. Bob really does get into a state. How he coped with the World Cup pressures I'll never know. It is a source of amusement to most of the Welsh boys to see one of the finest locks in the world transformed into a neurotic wreck over the most trivial of decisions. But what a tourist! Sadly, he was to break a shoulder during the first test, when he was playing in such commanding form.

There were a few other protests during the tour, but none to warrant much media attention. We certainly didn't feel anything like the intense pressures of Mike Gatting's ill-fated tour, and cocooned in hotels or rugby grounds few of us were aware that the few days spent in South Africa were anything but a rugby tour.

Back home, it was a different situation. At Port Elizabeth, where we had played our first game, Michael Boon, then of the *Express*, had become very excited about messages received from home. Our departure had catalysed a whole sequence of events which had dominated the headlines.

"Look at this," he called as he ran after us. "Rowlands has resigned!" A cutting from the *South Wales Echo* or some other paper was produced, and Boon could hardly contain his excitement at bringing us the news. Most of us appeared uninterested, thinking that the whole matter would blow over. Welsh rugby had lurched from crisis to crisis, and this one would be no different. Robert Jones, we knew, had phoned his father-in-law and WRU President, Clive Rowlands, on departure from Heathrow and was aware that Clive's resignation was on the cards. Perhaps it began to dawn upon us what the repercussions would be; yet that didn't for one moment persuade us that we had done anything wrong. It was a rugby tour undertaken by individuals, sanctioned by the IRB, with the invitations sent to us by the WRU. Yet Bob Norster wasn't convinced by such rationalisation and spent the next few days worrying.

With two test matches played and both lost, the tour was almost over. After the initial accommodation problems, we were left with pleasant memories of Cape Town, Pretoria and Port Elizabeth. It was a shame though, that the Welsh squad, playing alongside some of the world's best, hadn't realised their potential, and that "first off the plane game" had done us no favours at all.

Most of the Australian and French players stayed on in South Africa to visit the Kruger National Safari Park, whereas the Welsh had to find flights home. That was easier said than done since available seats were at a premium. Ann tried to organise, as best she could, a homeward journey for all; but the final seat allocations, I must admit, resulted in a few disenchanted members of the Welsh party. Paul "Tommy" Turner and his wife were given "economy" seats, and that didn't go down at all well.

My brother Andrew was at Heathrow ready to pick up Ann and me, and we managed to avoid the clutch of waiting reporters. However, on the journey towards South Wales we were told about the reception awaiting us. Most of us had been phoning home on a regular basis and had some kind of inkling of the media jamboree awaiting the South African travellers. We didn't have to wait long. I opened the front door after arriving at Pontlliw, got inside the house, only to hear the doorbell ring and to be greeted by a BBC reporter and film crew who fired questions without asking the time of day. This was only the beginning.

"Did you mean to embarrass the Welsh Rugby Union?"

"Are you now a rugby mercenary?"

"What eventually decided whether you should go or not?"

"What is your reaction to the resignation of the Welsh Rugby Union secretary, David East?"

"Did you act dishonestly?"

Question after question, phone call after phone call: they

69

would not leave us alone. The pressure was intense, and naturally the boys, now home, were getting very anxious indeed. My phone bill was phenomenal.

The WRU decided to appoint a panel of inquiry with a brief of "who, what, why, when and how much?" It was to be chaired by Vernon Pugh, QC. I still wonder about that. If the WRU wanted to know about the comings and goings of the South African tour, why didn't they ask their own committee members? Some of them had as much knowledge as anyone, particularly the IRB delegates, Gwilym Treharne and Terry Vaux.

The Union, no doubt, felt it was in the dock and had to be seen to act. The public, having been bombarded with daily media stories about players receiving money, and officials resigning, were not to be denied their daily ration of the latest WRU soap opera.

I was sent a questionnaire by Mr Pugh which I initially ignored. I had no time for such nonsense and considered it an intrusion. He wrote a strongly worded letter after a while, asking me to respond to the questions. He received a strongly worded reply, for I wondered what we as players were doing in the middle of a QC inquiry, when we had accepted an invitation to play rugby through the WRU offices. It was bizarre, farcical and made me feel very angry and antagonistic towards the people in power. The Union wanted scapegoats and had obviously attempted to distance itself from the whole mess. As players, we knew who would carry the can.

Eventually, we were asked to appear before the inquiry. Of course, the boys communicated with each other before appearing, but there was little of "well rehearsed replies" which were talked about when Vernon Pugh delivered his conclusions. Naturally, we compared notes, making sure of dates, times, personalities and what was written or said. Doesn't anyone, faced with an inquiry, trial or tribunal, do so? My greatest sadness was that as a Welsh international player I was being placed in the dock by my peers – and it was they who had originally caused the rumpus. The RFU had asked the England players to explain their actions before and after the tour and had concluded the matter with a curt press statement. That was the end of the affair. Not in Wales, where the politics of the game has as much appeal as a hard-won Triple Crown. It was a nightmare, and, of course, life at home and work suffered. There wasn't a single morning without reference to some shred of so-called evidence that had been discovered by the writer of an "exclusive"-labelled article.

R. H. Williams had long since resigned as a WRU committee member. David East had tendered his resignation as secretary because he felt that his office had been ignored and abused. Gwilym Treharne and Terry Vaux left the International Rugby Board as Welsh delegates. Clive Rowlands, after resigning, had somehow been reinstated. It was now the players' turn to face the inquiry. What was the charge?

For nearly two hours Robert Norster, Anthony Clement, Robert Jones and I sat in front of Vernon Pugh and his inquisitors. To say that we resented being there would be a great understatement. However, it appeared that the questions were based on the information that we had already given in written form. Each player was asked about why he went, who approached him or had passed messages and, the important question, whether we had been paid. The answer to the last question was the sole reason for our being there and the reply was that we had received a financial package which took into account time lost from work, a tour allowance and compensation for the hassle which we would undoubtedly experience. Ironically, I suppose, having to face the inquiry was part of it.

It was left at that; there was little animosity. In truth though, it has never been left at that. I doubt whether any international rugby player in any country has experienced anything so traumatic as the public examination experienced by the Welsh players. We stood accused because of the ineptitude of the Union and some of its elected officers. The invitation to go to South Africa had been passed on to us by the WRU and that should have been the end of the matter.

Vernon Pugh concluded his report and the clubs demanded that they should be allowed to examine the findings. By this time, Denis Evans had been appointed as secretary of the WRU and the testimony given by the players and the Union officers involved in the South African saga was eventually shredded. A report of the inquiry's conclusions was sent to the clubs and inevitably "leaked" to the press.

Were the French, English, Irish, Australians, New Zealand and Scots players subjected to such torment? No, it was the way of the Welsh to be seen to be conducting themselves in a right and proper manner. Our capacity to inflict damage upon ourselves was once again unsurpassed by any other nation.

6

Getting a Kick Out
of the Game

"What else do you do in the game?" my father asked.

"I just kick the ball," I replied.

He wasn't satisfied at all.

"What do you mean, you just kick the ball? They must want you to do something else? What position are you, for instance?"

"That's it," I told him, "It's the role of the specialist kicker."

I had just told my father of an approach by the Los Angeles Rams, the American Football team, who had invited me to consider joining them. I doubt whether he'd watched American Football at all, and he was clearly unimpressed by any game which demanded only one skill of a player.

Ironically, I knew what he meant because in rugby terms I would like to think that I have contributed a little more than a point-scoring boot. I'd be a rich man if I'd had ten pence for every time I've been introduced or referred to as "the Welsh kicker". I'm sure other sportsmen feel the same, particularly if they've spent countless hours on practising other skills.

If the full-back position in modern play simply demanded a custodian-style full-back – the last line of defence – and allied to that a dependable kicking ability, I wouldn't feel resentful. There is much more to the no. 15 jersey, and those who ignore those demands won't make it to the highest level. The law changes force the contemporary full-back to play a major part in a team's attacking strategy. The likes of J. P. R. Williams, Andy Irvine of Scotland and Sergo Blanco of France have rewritten the rules of engagement.

The full-back is now part of the defensive and attacking trio: he and the two wings. Each one has to help the other. This is why, much to the annoyance of some, I have always positioned myself close to the wingers. Either they or I will be responsible for the counter-attack if the opponents' kick fails to find touch.

There are others who feel that the full-back should lie deeper and more infield. Yet invariably the wing and the full-back will be the catalyst and the prompter of the next move, and I would rather be in the thick of the action than having to travel towards it.

Yet more important is to master the skills which are required of you: the fair catch, the safe kick to touch or the directional kick and making the tackle count. These are the grounding skills of a full-back at any level. We don't always succeed, but the intention must be to master them all. Ideally the full-back or any back should be able to kick with both feet, but few have mastered that. Paul Turner of Newport and Wales is the best example; I confess to having spent hours practising with my weaker left foot, but the right boot remains the solid favourite. The tight corner, especially at international level where the play is yards faster, requires both feet to get you out of trouble. It is the practice, and if the length is not what it should be, I wouldn't worry. No one will thank you for missing touch inside your own twenty-two metres.

At school and university I played at outside-half and I think that experience, especially under Stan Addicott at Swansea, taught me a great deal about positional play. It has helped me to read the opposition's intentions, watching their signals, the length of the pass and the player's first and favourite options. The more talented they are the more difficult they are to read, and this is why you must have trust in your wings to help you out when the unexpected chip or grubber kick comes your way.

I have missed tackles and have cursed, because as the last line of defence there are times when you only have one option and this is to take your man head-on. If the opportunity arises of forcing your man to a side tackling angle, then so much the better, provided you have the necessary speed to commit yourself. The more you make your opponent worry about his line of attack, the more time you allow for help to arrive.

Playing against Southern Hemisphere teams is that much more difficult since they use their second five-eighths to dictate play as much as the outside-half. It requires adjustments in your game and the ability to reach the angles of penetration. If you have the skills you must use them, but I have found that the most difficult skill of all is to maintain concentration at a peak for the full duration of the game.

You should be just as fast as your wingers, as robust as your centres and be able to read the game as well as your outside-half. All this from someone dubbed a "kicker"! Being called a reliable and consistent kicker has its burdens, too. You are not expected to miss easy kicks and if you do there's a gasp of horror on the terraces. Should you miss a sequence of kicks then according to the pundits on the terraces your career is over, you've been having too many late nights, and their grandmothers could kick better.

I have played in matches where other consistent goal-kickers have had nightmares. I recall Michael Kiernan and Brian Smith of Ireland, and Gavin Hastings of Scotland, and I've watched Michael Lynach and Grant Fox struggle Down Under. I take no pleasure in watching a player having one of those afternoons, and my only comfort is the knowledge that it can happen to anyone.

I remember taking an easy penalty for Neath against Sale right in front of the posts and about fifteen metres out – the kind of kick which Mark Ring could back-heel over the bar, and has done. From the corner of my eye the Neath scoreboard keeper was already notching up the extra three points. It was enough to break my concentration, and I missed.

Even worse is having a reputation for being successful with the long ones. There are so many variables in long-distance attempts, but people have expected them to sail over without any problem at all. I suppose I brought it upon myself with that one long kick against Scotland in 1986. Believe me, there are times when I wish it had missed. Every kick now has its burden. To this day, I don't really know why I attempted that one. I just fancied it. I asked David Pickering, the Welsh captain, for the ball and I think that most of the players, let alone the crowd, thought that I was going to punt for the corner.

David muttered, "But it's seventy yards." There was a slight swirling breeze against us at the time but the wind had been backing us for most of that half. That is another thing the terraces don't fully appreciate. The Arms Park at ground level is sometimes a mini-tornado. The flags flutter in all sorts of directions. I felt, though, that I'd have enough help to achieve the distance. I knew I was capable, since I'd kicked a few long ones for both Ebbw Vale and Neath. When you feel right, you know it, and on that day everything was OK.

"You must be joking," I heard one of the players mutter behind me as I placed the ball some ten metres inside the Welsh half as the Scots players, probably just as incredulous as my own team, lined up. The usual routine was observed, which has only slightly altered over the years: place the ball in an upright position, identify a mark on the ball, take four steps back, wipe the nose on the sleeve (disgusting habit for television viewers), turn sideways with left shoulder towards posts and take a last look at the target. Some kickers aim at a face in the crowd or a flag, as an aid to identifying a true line of direction. I have always gone for the posts.

The similarities between goal-kicking and striking the ball in golf have always fascinated me. The Ballesteros and Palmer books always tell you to keep to a routine, always concentrate but don't be too tense. It's exactly the same in penalty kicking. If you are too tense, then the kick will probably turn out to be a duffer. Lines and angles have to be obeyed and the follow-through, but I don't advocate the wiping of your nose on a sleeve in the British Open. I was totally relaxed when taking that kick.

The run was a normal one but I knew I had to give it a fair old thump. The connection with the ball would have to be clean. People have asked me countless times if I had thought it would go over before striking. That wasn't really the point. Even if it had gone close, Scotland would probably have cleared to touch with Wales having the throw-in closer to the opposition try line. It was just worth the gamble.

Away she went, and for a moment I thought the kick was drifting slightly to the left. Ah well, too bad! So I turned to cover the touchline, just in case we were able to launch a counter attack.

Then suddenly there grew that unmistakable roar of approval. It's strange, but I swear you could stand outside the Arms Park and have a fair idea of what was going on inside from the noise generated by the crowd. A mild applause invariably signifies a good kick to touch, with half of the crowd thinking that the running option should have been taken. A passing movement which gathers pace and penetration invites sporadic roars, and there's no mistaking the swell of disappointment. The roar grew and I turned too late to see the ball creep over. "A monster of a kick," I believe Bill McLaren said upstairs. It had been drawn towards the posts. It was, of course, a moment of sheer delight, and I turned to salute Dad and Andrew somewhere in the South Stand and left the statisticians and Bill McLaren to sort out the distance. Meanwhile my mother knew nothing of this. She had decided that the tranquillity of a drive with an aunt on Gower was far more appealing than the nervous tension of an international. The tape was brought out later by that jovial crowd the Arms Park ground staff, and it measured 70 yards 8½ inches. From that moment on I was expected to kick penalties from everywhere. Yet I don't believe it was the longest of the day.

Some day, after a careful examination of a video of that game, I will take a tape along to the Arms Park and with the help of Tony Horne and the boys measure the second distance penalty which went over. It was again a fairly straight attempt and the ball was still very high as it went over the bar, although the press boys gave it as 53 metres. That kick gave me more satisfaction than the first because it gave us a winning margin against Scotland. All kicks give you a measure of satisfaction when they go over but to be truthful I prefer the long belters because, despite what people say, I feel less pressure than when confronted with a 15 metre sitter. Since you are Mr Reliable and Mr Consistent you are under a remit to get those over!

That word "pressure" is so often used and so often misunderstood. It's no wonder I'm going bald, because I have felt that every kick has been vital for Wales in recent years. As things stand, the penalty or conversion decided so many matches. I am not convinced, as I mention elsewhere, by the arguments that it should be devalued, although I favour any law changes to make the game more expansive. There are, of course, different pressures when taking kicks. The more vital they are to the cause, the bigger the pressure. Strangely, I am not aware of it once the decision has been taken to go for the posts. I only feel that when I watch the videos at home. Two kicks especially have given me enormous pleasure, and both were vital for Wales.

In 1988 under Bleddyn Bowen's captaincy, we had already beaten England and Scotland and we travelled to Ireland in search of a Triple Crown, that imaginary piece of jewellery which has proved to be so elusive for Wales in the 1980s. The Irish as ever gave us a tremendous fight. There was little pattern to the game; there hardly ever is in Dublin. The wind destroyed any aspirations we might have had of a running game and Jonathan Davies had one of those days when nothing would go right. I don't know how many drop-goal attempts he missed, but it was all in desperation with little composure. Ireland were leading 9–3 at half-time and once again looked set to deny Wales any honours that season.

Though we had the wind in the second half, it made little difference. Gradually, though, we crept back into the game and I was given a penalty with a few minutes to go from the touchline with the scores level at 9–9. Naturally, I knew what was at stake and so did the rest of Lansdowne Road. Apart, that is, from my father. All in all he didn't have a good weekend. Before the match he'd been mistaken for one of those rough, uncouth Welsh supporters in a fashionable shop by my mother-in-law's friend, and the weekend went downhill from there.

He misses very little, but he didn't have any idea of how

important a moment it was going to be. For some reason, I think it was those annoying railway gates at Lansdowne Road, his entry into the ground was delayed and he failed to get a good vantage point. Having missed the beginning of the game and with no scoreboard in view he was always one score behind. So when the award was given, my father was under the impression that it was for a tie and not a win. He later commented that he thought the Welsh supporters rather enthusiastic for a kick which made matters level! He's taken some ribbing for that, I can assure you.

"Put this one over," said Bleddyn as he handed me the ball. Easy for him, no mean penalty kicker himself, but I wonder whether he would have fancied it? I'd already missed four penalties so I knew I had to do something. After all, I knew that most people thought I'd only been brought back into the team for my kicking ability after the injury to Anthony Clement. It was a matter of concentrating once again on the basics, of lining the ball correctly, head down and a good strike. I knew that I'd tried too hard with the other shots, over-compensating for the wind. Michael Kiernan had probably done the same.

With this one, though, I knew it was there the moment I'd struck it, and the crowd behind confirmed that it was a good and accurate flight. I didn't bother waiting for the touch judges; the moment was sheer relief after the earlier attempts. It shouldn't have been so crucial but it was. Once it was over, there was no way Ireland were going to come back, physically or psychologically. It was that warm feeling of being a member of a Triple Crown side, despite leaving the outcome to be decided a little late in the day.

Relief? Of course there was. It was a moment to savour for the rest of my life. Yet, strangely enough the dressing room was subdued. It was a win, of course, and a Triple Crown victory, but we sat there, heads down, since we knew that the quality of the game had been poor. On a personal note I remember hugging Tony Gray, our coach, the man who had dropped me that season. It was relief that I had come through and not let the team down, but I'd also proved a point to myself – and to others, as well.

Moments like these are treasured memories: they cannot

be taken away from you no matter what is written or said. In that light, it has been slightly irritating, whenever the '87 World Cup has been talked about, to be applauded for the touchline kick that won Wales third place in the tournament. I was delighted to have got that one over, and of course it's my favourite kick. So much depended upon it, and we returned home with something after our total demolition by the All Blacks.

Yet I think my biggest contribution to that game against Australia was the hand-off on Nick Farr-Jones and the pass to Adrian Hadley in the corner for the try. Without the try there wouldn't have been the kick. I suppose I will have to live with it – Thorburn the kicker.

The delight of seeing that one go over has not been matched. The first World Cup for Wales has been a bit of a curate's egg. We hadn't been fancied by the pundits to achieve much after the qualifying rounds and for me, having missed most of the previous season with another shoulder injury, it provided the perfect stage for international rehabilitation. The tournament was an immense challenge to all – players, coaches, administrators, journalists and broadcasters. Strangely, I don't think we'll see its like any more, since the event is inevitably going to become more commercial and more removed from the Saturday touchline supporter.

Those memories of travelling between New Zealand and Australia, Invercargill on a Sunday, our scrum-half Ray Giles with seventeen "air-shots" on the first tee at Rotorua –they were forever etched on the mind. Of more importance, and that is why the final kick against Australia means so much to me, is that I thought it would give Wales the opportunity of revitalising our approach back home.

We had come third in the world in the inaugural World Cup and that, if nothing else, ensured respectability. We had beaten Canada, Tonga, Ireland, England and Australia to achieve that status. Fine, and I can see Clive Rowlands beaming with pleasure. The problem is that I can recall his answer in a press conference when we had been taken to the cleaners by New Zealand and dumped 49–6.

"Where does that leave Welsh rugby?" asked John Mason of the *Daily Telegraph*.

80

"We go back to beating England every year," came Clive's reply.

Much as Clive has done for Welsh rugby in the many offices that he's held, his answer underlined the deep-rooted parochialism that has thwarted any kind of expansive thinking since the days of the late Carwyn James.

Meanwhile, outside the press tent at Ballymore, John Dawes, who was then the Welsh national coaching advisor, was shedding a different light on our predicament. He told reporters, "It is the refusal of officials to accept that we have been overtaken and still think we are leaders that has been much of the curse for our slide. In a nutshell, we are light years behind in fitness, strength and determination. We have got four years before the next World Cup to get it right."

I wonder whether it was pure coincidence that Clive stayed on in the Union to become president and manager of the Australian tour, whereas John Dawes was sacked. Be that as it may, the lessons were not absorbed. We didn't go back to beating England every year. In fact, four national coaches later, we were again thrashed by New Zealand and Australia and had lost every game to France. It is difficult to accept, but we have to, that we are a pretty unreceptive bunch.

Such feelings never entered my mind on that afternoon at Rotorua when lining up that kick. We played our hearts out against Australia, who had been limited to fourteen men after the sending-off of David Codey. The Australian captain, Andy Slack, attempted to belittle our win afterwards because of the sending-off, but I've always maintained that we could have won on even terms that afternoon. That is not to say that we were the better team; but Wales on that particular afternoon wanted desperately to win and I suspect that Australia were not as determined. You often find that at international level. One team sometimes appears to want to win more than the other. I suppose it's a question of mood.

Yet in kicking that conversion, did I do Wales a disservice? Did it convince some that we were really Number Three in the world? It was an achievement, there's no question about that, but did it also invite complacency? I suspect it did, for nothing changed. In fact, we ignored the rout at Ballymore and toasted Rotorua instead.

Richard Moriarty, our captain in the World Cup, thinks that our performances in the World Cup will stand the challenge of time. He's probably right, since we were plagued by injuries and the planes heading for London were full of injured Welshmen. I only wish we'd opened our minds to reality a little more, and accepted that in world terms there was New Zealand, and the rest of us were merely extras. The lesson was not lost on the likes of Australia and, to some extent, England and Scotland. It should have been our warning not to be left behind.

Within that four years we struggled to beat British Columbia, Canada and Namibia and lost to Romania. That was the reality of not having absorbed what the New Zealanders were only too pleased to teach us. The kick went over, and we were third in the world.

Having a reputation as a kicker has had mixed blessings. After the measured penalty against Scotland, I found myself that summer looking after security at one of the Royal Welsh Showground tents in Builth Wells. Gerald Davies approached me and told me that a contact of his who had a link with the Los Angeles Rams would like to meet me. Gerald told me that it could lead to an offer if I was interested. I'd seen the game on television and like so many Channel 4 viewers, I'd become fascinated by it. Interested? Of course I was, and I phoned Gerald's "contact", London Welsh vice-president, John Rendall, as soon as I could. He told me that the Rams were coming to London during the summer and would be playing the Denver Broncos in a promotional game at Wembley Stadium.

My first thought was to clear myself with the Welsh Rugby Union just in case I was in danger of breaching my amateur status. No problem there, said the then secretary, Ray Williams (as it is considered a different game), so I allowed John Rendall to do all the negotiating. I knew they were serious when suddenly twelve American footballs arrived at home with a tee which they use for all floor kicks. I practised quite a bit, only too aware that there would be a pretty large crowd at Wembley and an even bigger one on television. I did not want to make a fool of myself. The big day arrived when I was to meet my new team-mates at a practice session at Crystal Palace. They were monsters. Nice monsters, mind you!

I quickly realised that you have to be an exceptional player to make the squads of the professional clubs. This was made abundantly clear to me when I was asked if I'd be interested in joining. First, a contract was put in front of me which I had to sign. It was a "rookie" contract, basically a form of insurance cover, but it was worth $70,000. It's amazing how the mind concentrates when you are looking at a row of noughts.

The offer did appeal to Ann and me, as we contemplated living in the United States. However, there was a small matter of impressing the Rams and their owner, Mrs Georgia Frontiere.

The first practice session was at Crystal Palace and I was conscious of the fact that there were a few reporters present. I didn't want publicity at this stage, although everything had been cleared at the WRU.

Gradually the kicking coach, one of several specialist people on the coaching team, increased the distances of the kicks. It was going rather well, I thought, and then we did some punts. The aim was to kick the ball downfield some sixty yards, allowing the ball to stay in the air for four seconds. So far, so good.

On the second snap the ball was fired back and I noticed this rather large frame coming towards me. It was enough to put me off completely, since I knew he didn't want to ask me about the British weather. The kick was sliced and the ball hit a blocker's helmet. It was greeted with some mirth.

After the session one of the reporters recognised me, and I knew that this little venture would cause some comment at home, especially from my father. The fact that I was actually considering the offer was perplexing to him, especially when he realised that for a fortune, all that was required from me was kicking the ball.

The big day arrived after we'd spent some time with the Rams at their no-expense-spared hotel. They were kings, and I'll never forget their superb evening outfits at a dinner and dance arranged a few nights before the Wembley match. They looked superb, a million dollars, which was probably what some of them were earning.

My only brief was to get the game going with the kick-off. I'd been told that if the scores allowed, I'd be called in for a kick or two. Fat chance. The game was for real, less charitable than a Neath–Aberavon friendly.

On I went, padded up to the nines, helmet on, and teed up the ball. Unfortunately, they had spelt my name incorrectly on the back of the jersey. Instead of "Thorburn", it read "Thurburn." but I couldn't care less. They did, and a man was sent to round off the "U" into an "O". I was a nervous wreck and it turned out to be one of my worst kicks ever. It hardly rose, and upstairs the American commentator was having a field day.

"Thorburn kicks but it's not a good one. Seventy thousand dollars for what?" he asked himself. He was entitled to his disbelief, since it was a pretty poor effort.

Unknown to me at that time, the Neath boys were on tour in the States and watching the game. They didn't know of my American Football escapade, but there they were in a Florida hotel watching my Wembley début and débâcle. When they saw the kick and heard the comments, I don't think there was a dry eye in the house.

As soon as the game finished, the Rams and Broncos headed for Heathrow airport and home. Ann and I headed west and stayed in a Swindon hotel just off the M 4.

They had told me that if I was interested I should get in touch with them. I haven't as yet, and at least it wasn't one of those "we'll call you, don't call us" messages. It still appeals to me, but they've probably forgotten Thurburn by now.

7

"Get Your Passport"

Whether rightly or wrongly, I have often felt like an outsider. Not aloof, I hope, but not quite a part of the Welsh scene. When I arrived, almost unannounced, to play first-class rugby at Ebbw Vale, no one knew who I was and it was only on the recommendation of someone else that I began playing at the Eugene Cross ground.

There were only a few games at the end of my term at Swansea University and the travelling was too much, particularly as I had no car.

Having taken stock of the situation, I moved to the Gnoll where the incumbent full-back, Neale Harris, had already established a fine points-scoring record with 299 for that season. Much to the chagrin of the Neath club, and Brian Thomas in particular, Neale joined South Wales Police, for whom he had to play, and the berth was open to all challengers.

It was going to be my first full season. Yet I felt a little alien to the situation. Here were players who had been capped at some school or youth level and they all seemed to know each other. It didn't matter whether they came from Neath or not. In the after-match functions, the Swansea, Cardiff and Llanelli players seemed to be on first-name terms, not that it mattered a farthing when they were out on the field. That was different, because old scores had to be settled and new ones established.

Within that Welsh claustrophobia there is a true affinity. The backgrounds are similar, the environment the same. Mine was not, and it was a far cry from the disciplined world of a dormitory at Hereford or the comfort of home while at Swansea University. It would take time; not that players like Paul Jackson and Alun Edmonds or Steve Powell would allow you any modicum of consideration. Show a weakness now, I told myself, and they'll have you. My accent was different, as well. Somehow that slight feeling of alienation made me that much more determined to succeed and be accepted, if not on level terms socially, then certainly on the field.

I could not have wished for a better first season. Half-way through I had broken Neale's record and the club was climbing to its highest position in the Unofficial Championship in fifteen years. It was the beginning, and with eighteen tries I was satisfied that I was contributing a little more than a reliable boot.

It was the season of the Australian Grand Slam team who thrilled everyone with their quicksilver handling of the ball, and also a winter of freezing temperatures. The cold weather forced a reshuffle of fixtures and that helped me enormously in achieving one of the most treasured ambitions of any rugby player, that of playing for your country. England and France were to be met later in the season, which gave me an opportunity of capturing a few eye-catching headlines, let alone a decent number of points. Had the matches not been postponed I don't know whether the selectors would have gambled with me at that time.

There were so many peaks during that season. "Who recalls Harris now?" asked Lewis Stuart in his local paper, and John Billot, who blows hot and cold, headlined one of his articles in the *Western Mail*, "Thorburn looks the man for Wales". It was all very comforting, and in a "B" international against France at Newport I managed to contribute seventeen points in a 29–20 victory. It is interesting to note some of the names in that France "B" team: players such as Eric Champ, Henri Sanz, Marc Andrieu and Denis Charvet were also at the doorstep of long international careers.

Wales lost heavily to the all-conquering Australians in the autumn, and then came the freeze. So when the Five Nations Championship matches resumed, the entire schedule had been altered. Scotland were defeated, and it was the turn of the Irish to visit Cardiff. It was a game dominated by the boot, and poor old Mark Wyatt of Swansea, one of the nicest men around in rugby circles, had a dreadful afternoon. Whereas he had kicked fourteen points at Murrayfield in a 25–21 win for Wales, he only managed one penalty against Ireland; Michael Kiernan, on the other hand, kicked thirteen points. In one day, out the other. I know the feeling only too well.

Although I was in the Welsh squad I hadn't given any thought to being selected for my country. Concentration was being fully applied to keeping my place at Neath. Besides there were other full-backs around: Gwyn Evans of Maesteg, a British Lion, Howell Davies of Bridgend, and the gifted Martin Gravelle of Llanelli.

I wasn't there when the phone rang, but the late Rod Morgan, chairman of selectors, had left a message with my brother Andrew for me to call him back.

"Congratulations," he said, "Get your passport and brush up on your French."

"Am I on the bench?" I asked.

"No, you're in the team," he replied. He said something else after that, but I haven't a clue what it was. He might just as well have read the Kama Sutra backwards for all I knew. It was a dream, unreal: a whole stream of thoughts flooded in, and I had that nervous, tingling feeling. My father's words at Hereford came back to me: "One day you'll play for Wales."

We rang a few friends, and the traditional celebrations began at a local pub. Brian Thomas came down and the night was long. It was another of those emotional gatherings for which the Thorburns are famous.

There was one slight problem: I'd been selected for the Welsh students against the French Universities in Paris that weekend. They'd have to find a new full-back – their problem, not mine. I was going to play for Wales.

I wish life had been a little slower that week so that I could remember what happened. It seemed like a never-ending series of phone calls and bewildering excitement. The family, proud as punch, approached the visit to Paris with military precision – timetables, phrase books, maps and a quick check on the exchange rate. It was going to be some family outing. Neil, my brother, on service somewhere in darkest Bavaria, would make his way on an European train which would arrive in Paris in time. Tickets had to be found somewhere, by someone, somehow. A letter arrived from the Union informing me that I would receive one complimentary ticket and three others which would cost me £20 each. Would I make sure I had the money on me at the next training session!

Before I knew it I was on the Welsh team flight to Paris to play against the likes of Blanco, Sella, Esteve and many more who had been mere names on past programmes and mispronounced on *Rugby Special*. I held on to the card signed by Ray Williams, the Welsh Rugby Union Secretary, inviting me to play. No, it wasn't a dream, it was for real.

The gathering, the flight and the trip to the team hotel are a mere blur. I was too young to know what to do, too young to appreciate what was happening.

We lost the match, but I don't think I let the side down, since the press reports were favourable. I kicked one penalty, missed one, and hit the post with another, but the French scored two tries through Esteve and Jerome Gallion and were, despite our missed chances, in another sphere of operation. As ever, one player caught my eye. No matter how inspiring Mark Ring was on that day, and he tried everything, Serge Blanco was as unpredictably productive as ever. The French stopped us from scoring and their line was unbreachable that season. For me, it was over before it had begun and I knew I had to conquer my nervousness under the high ball. It was all I could register in the bewilderment of so much excitement.

Some factors emerged immediately. There was no sympathy out there for a newcomer and the French crowd, as I was to learn, were an uncompromisingly vocal lot. Robert Ackerman, my first international room-mate, had warned me about this, but there is no substitution for first-hand experience. The speed of it all had been dazzling, and I've yet to live through a quicker afternoon. It was over. I couldn't believe it. I had tried to convince myself that I was

LEFT: *Wales World Cup Squad 1987*

*In action for Wales in 1990 (*ABOVE*) and in 1991 against Ireland (*LEFT*)*

OPPOSITE TOP LEFT: *Most speeches were written on a napkin*

OPPOSITE TOP RIGHT: *Gunning for $70,000 with the L.A. Rams*

OPPOSITE BELOW LEFT: *A WRU pro-celebrity golf tournament. Why do they ask me?*
dislocated shoulder, broken collarbone, cortisone injections

OPPOSITE BELOW RIGHT: *Haven't they heard? Discovering the Namibian "rough"*

ABOVE: *En route to South Africa*

BELOW: *The International XV squad in South Africa*

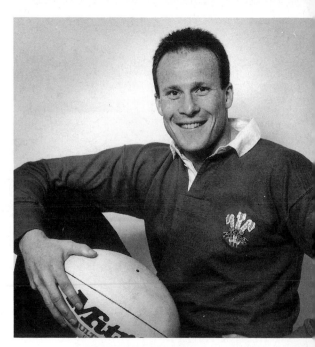

RIGHT: *One last smile*

BELOW: *The Thorburn*
masterplan. First a
Welsh cap, then a career

going to enjoy the experience, but the final whistle had gone before I remembered such intentions.

It was also my introduction to French post-match dinners. The family were having adventures of their own, being entertained by hosts prepared to present them with sixteen-course meals, Andrew's conservative estimate; then Ann lost her handbag and subsequently hated every minute of the weekend.

Meanwhile, one-cap wonder was sitting down to bottles of Moët Chandon and taking in everything, including the champagne. It wouldn't have bothered me if that had been my only cap, because "one-cap wonder" or not, it can't be taken away from you.

Terry Holmes, the captain from Cardiff, mentioned me in his speech. That was pretty decent of him and I've always tried to do the same with new caps. He referred to the fact that I'd won my first cap as a twenty-one-year-old, whereas he'd been a few months older when he received his in Australia.

There was that feeling of warmth. When I got home, the family were still in transit from France, and by the time Ann returned, I was in bed, shattered by the whole experience.

I suppose I had done well enough, since I was named in the Welsh team to play England at Cardiff a fortnight later. It was fairyland time for me, less so for Gareth Davies, the Welsh outside-half. The selectors wouldn't name a no. 10 and insisted that Gareth play for Cardiff against Malcolm Dacey of Swansea in a club match on the weekend prior to the England game so that they could come to a fair and objective decision. It was utter nonsense, since it was already April because of the postponements and if the selectors didn't know the merits of either player by then, several thousand Welsh spectators – able selectors if required – did. Gareth promptly, and rightly in my opinion, told the selectors what he thought of them and departed from the squad.

Man management has never, in my opinion, been the forte of the WRU officials. There seems to have been little consideration, and on occasion players have heard of their selection on radio, or read their names in newspapers.

Having been dropped twice during my international career, I speak from bitter experience. The first time there was no warning. The team was announced in the Welsh changing room with the entire Welsh squad present. No explanation, no reasons given, nothing. You just stared at the floor unable to look anyone in the face, and then you were expected to go out and give your all as training fodder for the selected ones. At least on the second occasion John Ryan did tell me beforehand that they wanted to try Anthony Clement at full-back to give them greater options, but still didn't give me an explanation of why I deserved the blade. I would like to think that matters will improve, but I fear that in the pecking order of television, radio, newspapers and leaks, the player will inevitably come last.

Ultimately the selectors did not opt for Malcolm Dacey at outside-half against England, but sprang a surprise on everyone by naming our Neath outside-half Jonathan Davies for his first cap. It was also to be my first experience of Cardiff Arms Park on international day and the all-enveloping atmosphere of a home Welsh International.

The Welsh team headquarters was at St Mellons Country Club, a converted mansion on the outskirts of Cardiff. Despite the comfortable surroundings it might as well have been in the Orkneys as far as atmosphere went. There was little to do and therefore nothing to distract anyone. Some coaches believe this to be beneficial. Not me. I would prefer the buzz of the game to be around me, to underline the importance of the event. We had some entertainment but not the kind you'd expect!

Jonathan and I were having a quiet game of table tennis, whereas the Neath hooker, Mike Richards, and Pontypool's scrum-half, David Bishop, were at the pool table. Suddenly all hell broke loose as David accused Mike of potting the wrong ball, and it was no friendly accusation, either. The confrontation, with temperatures soaring by the second, was eventually resolved, with Jonathan and me shaking at the roots.

I have never been able to understand David Bishop. He was probably one of the most talented players of my era. Sadly, allied to his single-minded approach to the game, was a self-destructive and impulsive nature. Strong-willed and deceptively quick, he could destroy teams single-handed and dominate scorelines. Unfortunately some people were uncomfortable in his company. Paul Jackson of Neath was the only man who could meet him on equal terms in our confrontations with Pontypool's "Bish". Not much bread was broken between those two, I can tell you, and the discussions were not about the pros and cons of Page Three girls.

"Bish" once did a jig and a wiggle for the television cameras at Pontypool during a cup match against Swansea. He'd kicked a magnificent penalty from the mud and his celebration dance was captured for all to see. I watched it at home and decided that if the opportune moment came, I'd do the same. A bit silly, of course, and the sages of yesteryear would probably frown. Let them. The game lacks levity, or so everyone tells me. My opportunity came when we met Pontypool, and David Bishop, at Cardiff. One of my kicks went over and the impulse took me. I did a wiggle, to camera of course, and felt a real twit. Funny thing is, the "Bish" hasn't mentioned it at all. I didn't think it was that bad an impression. Perhaps that was the problem.

The pool table incident apart, little else did happen at St Mellons and I was grateful when the WRU decided to bring the team back into Cardiff city centre before internationals. Only on the Saturday morning when the team bus drove into Cardiff from the country hotel were we aware of the day's major event. Before kick-off I went off to the toilet to memorise the words of "Hen Wlad Fy Nhadau", which my mother had kindly written out for me. It's still a bit of a struggle getting the words out, but I was all right if one of the Welsh speakers, Kevin Phillips or Ieuan Evans, was next to me.

Again, the match against England was fast and often too furious. With a changed back row and a better scrum we were more comfortable winners than the scoreline of 24–15 suggests. Jonathan announced his arrival on the international scene with a try and a dropped goal. Chris Martin had failed to gather one of Jonathan's high kicks, leaving it to bounce, and the Trimsaran whippet was in. As the fury of the battle got a little tempestuous with Mons Palmade heavily employed as arbitrator and umpire, the penalties also came flowing. At the end of the day I had a satisfying tally of thirteen points, three penalties and two conversions, plus a kick from inside our half which hit the post.

I was well pleased. I had come through the test without any serious mishaps. There are some internationals who have played for Wales, but not at the Arms Park. Peter Francis was one who deputised for Stuart Evans at Murrayfield, and Aled Williams, Stuart Parfitt and Owain Williams were capped in Namibia. Who knows, their time may come again – and hopefully in front of home support.

There is nothing to compare with an Arms Park inter-national. Forget all those formal labels such as the National Stadium, or the National Ground. To generations past and future, it has been and always will be Cardiff Arms Park. The Cardiff club may have something to say about that, but throughout the world people talk and romanticise about our ground and I've yet to hear an Aussie or All Black call it the National Stadium.

Its location is within the heart of Cardiff's city centre. You see its stands towering over the River Taff, a concrete guardian over the national game. Granted that the Welsh soccer team, who have now moved in as neighbours, have enjoyed remarkable success there in recent years; but it will always be on loan, I hope – may they never be joint owners.

That central location is one of the ground's most attract-ive qualities. On international days it is the hub of the city as the droves park anywhere, anyhow, for the sometimes ticketless walk into Westgate Street. Though it is much changed from the days of the wooden North Stand and the times when Glamorgan used to play County Championship cricket next door, with the greyhounds racing at the final whistle, it still retains its magnetism for players. The singing may have declined, with so many arriving late after their rushed pints, or probably gin and tonics these days, but the National Anthem is still nerve-racking for visiting teams – and for some of us!

I sometimes think that before the WRU embarked on its redevelopment there could have been a more adventurous plan. It was probably lack of money, since the now much sought-after debentures were ridiculously cheap. The successful team of the 70s changed all that. With so much ground available the Arms Park could have been turned into a National Sports complex, housing not only rugby and soccer internationals, but also cricket, tennis and covered games courts. It could well have been the envy of every country. As it is, it's a fine stadium, and next door that wise old sage, Albert Francis, has transformed the Cardiff ground into the finest in the land.

Outside these grounds on an international morning, crush records are broken on an hourly basis at the neighbouring pubs. The bouncers stand guard knowing that humour is the best policy, since there are too many front rows and locks around. The search for tickets is a cry from the heart.

"Any spares?"

"Any swaps?"

"A South for a North."

"The Day of Judgement is Nigh!"

"Programmes!"

"Hundred quid for a stand!"

The sound of feet shuffling along Westgate Street, the odd call when an old friend is spotted, a bugle and a moving mass of red. The windows from the Angel Hotel look down on a nation on the move. Everything is red. Faces, scarves, hats, jerseys, coats, banners from Tylorstown, Cardiff Meds and even a large red banana.

The player is not immune to this. For years the team headquarters was the Angel Hotel, neatly positioned at the head of Westgate Street, a main meeting place, haven of touts, hangers-on, autograph hunters, WRU officials and us, custodians of numbered jerseys for the day.

There has been little sleep for some of us. Since arriving on Friday afternoon the weekend has already followed the pattern laid down on WRU tablets of stone. Friday night is cinema night, with Tudor Jones, the physiotherapist, entrusted with the tickets, popcorn and ice-cream kitty. The film has got to be gory, funny and unromantic. The

Welsh teams of the past when visiting Twickenham used to go to the pantomime, or if in Paris it had to be the *Folies Bergère*. That has changed. Blood, guts and a simple plot to the film are now the primary requirements, so that the forwards can follow, and discuss.

The walk back from the cinema is fraught with danger. There are early arrivals in Cardiff, and they've done all they can to spoil the weekend party by attempting to drink the pubs dry. Some of them are in a shocking state.

"Got a ticket butt? Isshh all right fer yew innit? You don' 'ave to pay to gerrin, do ya? Hey, Dai. Yunno who this is? Go on, 'ave a guess Dai. Isshh Mike 'All, innit?"

A quiet withdrawal to the Angel and a mental note to check in the mirror to see if I look remotely like Mike Hall. A few phone calls to check on the Thorburn ticket situation since there's invariably a panic, a last-minute request. Tea and sandwiches and an optimistic yawn. Fat chance of a good sleep, though. As captain there are so many things to think about, and I wish they'd stop that bloody singing downstairs. For Angel Hotel read Royal Albert Hall – without the organ.

The international day dawn beckons. Some have slept, but it's easy to note the ones who haven't. They pick at their breakfast, fiddle with idle hands, have fixed-on smiles and hundreds of relatives. There is a brunch at around eleven-thirty so there is ample time, too much time, to think. They are the same thoughts that have dominated everything since Wednesday: the game, and how it will go.

The arrival of the Thorburns is a study of organised chaos. To the outsider they could well appear to be well-heeled ticket touts. It is mathematical bedlam. How many tickets, where are the extra ones, when are they arriving, how are they going to get through the traffic and how will we recognise the friend of a friend who rang last Tuesday in the hope of getting an enclosure? On an international morning it was best that I ignored the Thorburn Ticket Trauma.

Time gathers pace, and everybody who is ticketless knows you by your first name. It's the height of your popularity for the day and the decade. In a few hours they'll question your birthright. Some familiar faces in the crowd that I should know. I'm hopeless with names. I'd rather hide behind the reception hall pillars. I have done, several times.

Where's Ann? A quiet word – she knows about the stomach knots, the thin-lipped smile and how best to say nought.

The brunch is a hopeless quest for a settling stomach. Some have omelettes, others pasta, but Paul Knight will eat anything. There is a team meeting at one. Key words to be remembered ... Pride, Speed, Commitment, Support, Impact. I am not a rousing passion-raiser. Leave that to the coach.

The late John Bevan was methodical in his approach, so too was Tony Gray. John was invariably in a bit of a mood, but a brilliant reader of the game. It was difficult to approach Tony, since he rarely shared his emotions. Tactics, strategy and blackboards yes, but the speech would hardly rate a movement of the needle on the Clive Rowlands Richter Scale. The problem with Clive's speeches was that like so many summer television programmes, they were repeats of re-runs. The new caps would listen with undivided attention as each and every one of them was asked about his commitment to the cause. Fathers, mothers, wives, girlfriends, uncles, aunts and the whole street depended on us that afternoon. We could not let them down. There was also the "Calon" factor – or "colon" factor as some have called it – if the heart wasn't up to it, you should not have been there. In another age Clive would have been a crowd-pulling reformation preacher, or the last Prince of Wales after Llewelyn. Some of us would quietly think of what was to be done that afternoon. The calon was beating faster.

John Ryan stayed too short a time for players to really get to know him, which was a pity, but in the end if the players don't perform for a man, and they didn't for John, the reality is a cruel exit. Ron Waldron was plucked from Neath, and it is true that certain players did not take to his brash methods. I suspect that the political knives were sharpened well before our departure to Australia. By the time we returned they were lethal. Yet the newspapers were

95

united for this promotion when John Ryan resigned. They were united in calling for Ron's head a few months later. No wonder I don't bother ordering a newspaper!

The red jersey should be sufficient motivation for all. It is time to get going. It is only a short walk from the Angel to the ground but it takes an eternity. The throng is gathered outside. Cockney accents selling red scarves, the over-whelming smell of fried onions, a few wobbling at the knees after too much hospitality and still the search goes on for tickets. Desperation is in the air.

The kitbags are thrown on to the floor in the changing room. The pegs are numbered and the new kit is laid out: jerseys, shorts and socks. It's time to go out and to have a look at the pitch. It's a way of killing time and on goes the Walkman and a moment or two with Chris De Burgh.

A few have gathered inside the ground, dads with youngsters, blazered committeemen who haven't been invited to pre-match receptions; the terraces are pretty full as the cheer goes up when they spot familiar figures dressed in the Number Ones or tracksuits.

It's relatively pointless testing for the wind at Cardiff unless there's a mild hurricane on the charts. If it's a westerly wind it rushes through the Marathon Gate and there's a multi-directional swirl towards the River Taff end. An easterly wind blows over the terraces and is caught by the curving stadium. You'd best forget trying to read its strength. By kick-off it will have changed.

As a captain I have always preferred playing against the wind in the first half. There is some logic to this, since every team I've been involved with takes the best part of fifteen minutes to settle down, which gives you the wind advant-age for forty minutes in the second half when the limbs are not quite as fresh as when you started. Other captains choose otherwise.

Back into the changing rooms, and a quiet word with each individual. There is silence now, with an urgent determination to get matters right from the beginning. The comics, David Evans and Rowland Phillips, are quieter men now. Each one to his own responsibilities. We know each other pretty well and there is no need to state the obvious. Few are allowed inside the closed door and fewer into the intensity of those private moments. The breathing of fifteen individuals in that room is irregular. A few deep breaths, a widening of the chest and a wink at your neighbour. A few limbering-up exercises, a stretch of an old nagging injury, and it is time to go out.

The roar never fails to heighten the senses. They want you to win. The pundits will talk about style, grace under pressure, control and other meaningful terms. We want to win, and if we are a point ahead at the final whistle, that will be good enough.

The band in place, the opposing team's national anthem is played and ungraciously jeered. Make a point of apologising for that later in the day. Then it is the turn of "Hen Wlad Fy Nhadau". The Arms Park takes a deep breath and manages to stay at least three bars behind the military beat. Emotional? Who wouldn't be?

There is nowhere like it. There is probably more noise generated by the Parc des Princes crowd, though. An international there has all the trappings of a continental festival. The French are wily, since their pre-match arrangements involve terrorising the opposition. The bus ride from the hotel with police outriders clearing the Paris traffic is one of life's more frightening experiences. Horns blowing, lights flashing – there are times you dare not look out. The channel is cleared but by the time you arrive at the ground the knees have gone and your stomach doesn't belong to you. It is little wonder that the other Five Nations teams traditionally get a slow start against the French.

Parc des Princes has not been a happy ground for me apart from the delight of that first cap. On my second visit Serge Blanco crashed into me as I was fielding a high ball and I broke my collarbone. I vowed that if the opportunity came I would return the compliment by giving him as hard a tackle as I could. Catching him was the problem. I left the field in pain, and the disappointment was deepened since we were in the lead at the time by 9–3 in a match we eventually lost 9–16.

There wasn't a single win for Wales at the Parc des Princes during my career, nor for that matter at the Arms

Park against the French. In the end I suppose we were somewhat inhibited by them. The French, once in the lead, are a difficult team to contain. There is also that Gallic flair for the unexpected, with the likes of Sella, Lagisquet, Berbizier and above all Blanco to thrill the crowd with their genius.

My last visit to Parc des Princes ended in a convincing 36–3 defeat, with six tries being scored against us. It was a painful yet entertaining experience. We were simply outclassed in every department and the French toyed with our young, harassed team. It would have been nice to win there once, but it was not to be; and in the Cardiff matches, more often than not, only penalties kept us in contention rather than flair.

There's a similar ride with police outriders on the way to Lansdowne Road in Dublin. The ground has far happier memories, especially after the Triple Crown win in 1988 and a victory in my first ever visit there.

Why is it always mayhem against the Irish? They never lack passion, they simply exude it. The first twenty minutes against any Irish side has never been easy. Whatever they feed them in that changing room – I suspect it's iron filings – does the trick. There's not a moment to spare when playing against them. They have contributed so much to the game, but above all the ability at times to play well above themselves. The choice of players in Ireland is limited, the choice of courageous players is not. Many a time I have wished we had that kind of commitment, the ability to combine inspiration, dedication and effort. It can go a long way to hiding deficiencies.

The Irish are great men off the field, too. When the whistle blows, organised animosity stops. A night in Dublin is a serious attack on the liver and the larynx. Who can ever forget Mick Doyle, the hefty Irish coach, in the middle of the '87 World Cup suffering a "trifling" heart murmur and insisting it had nothing to do with a late-evening bet on the number of push-ups he could manage. The Irish play hard both on and off the field and I consider it an honour to list some of them as genuine friends.

For me, Scotland has always been the watershed

country. I waited long enough for my first experience of Murrayfield, which did not turn out to be a particularly happy one. We were unceremoniously dumped 21–9 and played badly. Altogether it was a disastrous season in 1989. The scoreline against Western Samoa on tour in Wales (28–6) sounds convincing, but the performance lacked any kind of conviction, and then John Ryan dropped me against Romania. Wales lost that match, the first defeat at the hands of a non-International Board country.

It is difficult to explain how a country, after a Triple Crown year, could change so dramatically. We lacked confidence in ourselves, and I must confess that being dropped didn't exactly thrill me. Even more inconsistent was my selection for the next game, at Murrayfield, as Welsh captain.

The press columns were giving us a real hammering, and at the end of the season Stephen Jones suggested in *The Sunday Times* that it might help Wales to take drastic action at administrative level if they were to lose against England. As I've already mentioned, it made me boil and I reacted in a manner which incensed all those around me.

Yet when Scotland came to Cardiff in our Triple Crown year, I would like to think that we provided some of the best Welsh rugby of recent years. It was a grand match for Jonathan Davies in our 25–21 victory; it was also the stage for Ieuan Evans, with his twisting run, to prove that he was a world-class winger with a side-stepping try which would grace the opening credits of any rugby programme. That day we played with pride, passion and penetration. Unfortunately, despite our win for the Crown in Ireland, it was also the last time we played with the kind of conviction required at international level.

It is only a thin line, the difference between insecurity and confidence. When Ron Waldron was appointed coach after John Ryan had resigned after our heaviest defeat ever against England, he probably thought that the Neath boys, nurtured on success, would perform better than players in losing teams. Commitment was not lacking when he selected his first team for Murrayfield in 1990. The defeat in that first-ever whitewash season simply showed that we lacked a player or two in vital positions. They were not around, and so Ron had no option but to rely on successful and fit players. At national level, as opposed to club level, the same players did not perform.

I have always believed Scotland to have the potential of a great side, ranking alongside the best in the world. They proved this by defeating Will Carling's over-confident team at Murrayfield for the Grand Slam. The back-row mechanics of Jeffrey, Calder and White are as good a combination as any. With Gary Armstrong and Craig Chalmers behind the scrum we are witnessing a combination in the Laidlaw and Rutherford mould. There seem to be fewer changes to the Scots teams than any other country, apart from Ireland. Of course, you have the Hastings brothers as well. What is more, they are gentlemen too – and, much like the Irish, delightful company.

Do the Scots and the Irish really feel the way a Welshman does when they play England? They claim they do, but I swear the Welsh heart beats a little quicker if the white jerseys are the next opponents. Perhaps it is to do with history, oppression, "Rape of the Fair Country", I do not know. There is one game you have to win, and that is against England.

After so many successful years against them the tide has turned, and on 19 January 1991 I was captain of the first Welsh team to lose against them in 28 years. One try and seven Simon Hodgkinson penalties. Will they carve it on my gravestone? It's been mentioned often enough. Past Welsh captains over that 28-year period have had nightmares thinking that the dishonour would be bestowed on them. They may rest peacefully for ever more.

I don't think it is the player's fault; it is more to do with their sycophantic press. An England win heralds a new dawn, a new awakening. Suddenly everything is right with the world when England are on top – almost as if their position as custodians of the game is beyond question. And make no mistake: England have had some very talented players. Paul Ackford is a favourite of mine, and you'll find no better competitors than Mike Teague and Peter Winterbottom. Behind the scrum too, I have admired Jeremy

Guscott and Rory Underwood; and if they'd retained the services of Martin Offiah goodness knows what they could have achieved. Collectively, however, they assume an arrogance which I'm sure is incentive enough for Wales, Scotland and Ireland to raise their game.

There is also an element of jealousy in all this. It seems that all the resources are at England's disposal. Only recently a schools and youth centre of excellence was opened in the Midlands, the funding of rugby development for schools and clubs is adequate and their players do seem to land some pretty comfortable jobs. You'll not find many unemployed players in the England squad.

There is no real reason why Wales couldn't be the same. It is a question of attitude and being blessed with vision. My record against England stands at: played 6, won 3, lost 3. Not nearly good enough.

Eventually, with the marketing of the World Cup, the appeal of the game will broaden. Then it will be difficult to refute the claims of other countries to be allowed into the inner sanctum of the International Rugby Board organisation. There is no reason why countries such as Romania, Japan, USA, Canada and a host of others should be prevented from joining that august body. Recognition is already on the way, but as in all things in the rugby world, alacrity is not recognised as a virtue.

We have to recognise that rugby is organised at different levels in various parts of the world. Even within the International Board there are huge variations, from the attitude of the conservative RFU to that of the almost open professionalism in France. The days of dictating edicts are over.

Wales in recent years organised two tours to Canada and Namibia. I was fortunate to be part of both, though my presence in Namibia owed more to economic necessity and the daily allowance than anything else. In fact, Wales were the first national team to visit Africa's newest country. As the Irish boys will testify, Namibia are a force to be reckoned with, and I fully expect them to qualify for the World Cup of '95. The open streets of Windhoek, where the tourist trinkets are laid out on the pavement, are a far cry

101

from Princes Street in Edinburgh on an international morning. Yet it is an opportunity to widen one's experience and to see another part of the world.

In the barren lands of the Namibian desert you had time enough to reflect on the matters most important to you. My mind was on matters back home: how to make a living and keep the mortgage payments on an even keel. There was a rugged beauty to that country that remains unsurpassed, but I'm afraid that if you are not a wildlife enthusiast there is little to keep you occupied.

I appreciate a number of the problems confronting the International Rugby Board in dealing with some countries. Certainly in Namibia there was an independent arrogance: they could do what they liked, and to hell with convention. The refereeing in local matches was diabolical, but it would have been regarded as impolite to mention such matters to the hospitable communities. There is a need to welcome the likes of Namibia into the international fold, so that they too will realise their responsibilities.

The same problem arose in Canada, but to a lesser extent. You can't really complain when a tour takes you through the Rockies and the delights of Vancouver's cosmopolitan population. The matches were tough enough, especially the game against British Columbia, which ended up in a brawl and a draw.

I would like to thank all those hosts for memorable times. I sometimes wish we had behaved a little better. There has often been an arrogant attitude, even in defeat, which is something that I've never understood. Learning to live with the qualifying rounds of the next World Cup might induce a touch of reality, but I doubt it. That parochial barrier is pretty well impregnable. The player who has been outwitted, outplayed and outgunned at international level is tomorrow's local hero in a club game. It is better, for some, to be kings within a small community rather than expose themselves to the demands of a major challenge.

We too have a great deal to learn about courtesy. Boasting about having played the game for so many years and arrogance about its place in the fabric of the Welsh community is inexcusable. Wales no longer owns the

game. We may have contributed to its spread, but it is now
the property of the world community. As it should be.

8

The Big, the Small and the Talented

The truth of the matter is that the Welsh are a diminutive lot. We don't breed big men, and anyone over six foot two walking along the high streets of South Wales is in danger of being hijacked into the nearest rugby club. Only an anthropologist could explain why we are so short as a race. Some are outwardly abrasive in overcoming such a minor physical defect and a Welshman in victory, as countless Englishmen will tell you, can become an awesome burden. We gloat in victory and find the nearest available excuse in defeat without reason or rationalisation.

There is that story of the small lone Celt challenging the advancing Roman army to a fight over the hill. Legion after legion went over the hill and were never seen again. The Celt kept appearing to challenge the now depleted Romans. After the very last legion had been sent over, a lone bloody survivor made it back to the Roman commander to utter his last words. "That isn't a Celt," he whispered, "it's a Welshman; and don't believe him, there are two of them."

I've met some people who would be quite prepared to believe that little tale, especially when it comes to discussing rugby football. "You never beat Wales", said a seasoned New Zealand international, "you only score more points than them." A truism that is reflected in our undiminished zest to be the small one to conquer the big guns.

They are to be found in every club corner: experts specialising in rugby football, but at the sound of a beer tap able to turn their attentions with profound expertise to discussions on the Russian economy, the greenhouse effect on the Welsh valleys and the hidden personality of Samantha Fox. These same individuals "were always there", though you suspect that life's entire navigation has taken them as far as bookie, pub and club with the odd visit to the doctor, are never wrong. They are the brigade of "Wassanames" or "Watchumukalits", in whom erudition is replaced by emotion and compromise by conviction. I mention our friends for a special reason. Every Welsh player of the 80s and 90s hates and despises them.

The conversation normally takes this shape. There is no shake of hand, there is no introduction, because they know you. A one-way conversation is fair game.

"You're not as big as I thought you were. We were 'aving an argument about your size the other night. I told them about six foot two, and I was only an inch out wasn't I? J.P.R. was bigger. Now there's a player . . . fearless. He could tackle a bus, that man could. We don't see tackling like that nowadays do we? I was telling the boys 'you've got to tackle' and the bigger they are the better, innit? I was in the corner at the Arms Park when he bumped that watchumukalit French winger into the stand. It was right in front of me, aye. Tremendous thump. No we don't tackle like we used to. Mind you, I blame the schools and the Government.

"We don't have the backs either. Remember Phil Bennett? He could turn a man out of his vest he could, aye, and what about Gareth Edwards? He's done all right out of the game hasn't he? And do you know what? I reckon the best of them all was Gerald Davies. If you gave Gerald the ball fifty yards out it was a certain try. He's my wife's fifth cousin you know. Through marriage, of course. Pity about the divorce, but it's something to say, innit?"

Then he promptly asks for an autograph on a sodden beer mat and the pen doesn't work. It is all too familiar.

The Welsh team of the 70s were an exceptional bunch. Rarely have so many talented players graced the Welsh stage at one time. I'm not altogether sure whether I appreciate being told about their success at every street corner, and the lack of victories in recent years has only heightened the profile of Edwards, Bennett, Davies, Dawes, J.P.R. *et al*.

They were my heroes too. Scrounging for tickets, pressed against barriers, it was a sheer delight to follow them around. That "little bit of magic" as Bennett has said so many times, was a magnet for us all. There were skills to applaud and there was courage to admire: a generation or two of individuals who would grace many a Best XV selection. More's the pity that because of the amateur laws players like Edwards, John and Bennett sold their tales and experience to publishers rather than developing the talents of youngsters. What a waste that has been. They should have been allowed to write their books but at the same time given the opportunity of passing on their knowledge and encouragement to the likes of me and the new generation. So much was lost, never to be regained.

Like the stadium which denied our clubs any financial assistance for a decade or two, the amateur laws denied Welsh rugby its premier marketing people. Most have been hauled into the media to examine and pontificate, and it's difficult to accept and understand why they have become so adept at turning the knife. They of all people should know how difficult it is out on that park, but before you've wiped a brow after an international, the experts with scalpel tongues are having their pound of flesh. Mind you, they've been helped by our lack of success.

I suppose you have to grin and bear it. I consciously decided not to buy newspapers a long time ago. Invariably, though, someone would walk up and say, "Do you know what John Billot said about Neath in the *Western Mail* this morning?" Not that I took much notice of what the man in question said, but when the third or fourth person in an hour had mentioned the said damaging article, I would go off to find a newsagent. Particularly annoying were the tabloids with that bent for the eye-catching headline, which only sometimes had any relevance to what had been said. The fiction merchants with a deaf ear to "off the record" appeals are a dangerous species.

There are sportswriters and news sportswriters and the

latter I would not touch with a Western Samoan oar. Their interest in sport is negligible; but give them a hint that all is not well in a club or a rumour that a player is a bit of a night-life merchant, and they will camp on doorsteps and sleep in cars. I don't know how professional soccer players cope with these people, and many a sporting hero has been destroyed by the leeches.

For my part, I have been hounded at work and phoned at every hour – and all this as a player of an amateur sport. Yet it is the articles written by the ex-players which hurt most, and the words expressed by ex-Welsh internationals are even more indigestible. The men who kept me in awe from the barriers have themselves created barriers.

Phil Bennett was at one stage giving me a hard time, and I complained to Jonathan Davies about it. I don't know if Jonathan had a word with him, but the carping became less acerbic. That was one way of dealing with the problem.

Above all of them Bobby Windsor, the old hooker from Pontypool, stands head and shoulders as the worst of the bunch. From tabloid to tabloid, depending on the whim and presumably the street value of such quotes, Bobby is willing to pontificate on any subject . . . full-backs from Germany, Welsh Rugby Union secretaries from Hong Kong and twenty-six-year-old marketing executives in charge of the game. He is no longer in danger of being taken seriously: that time has long passed.

Yes, I suppose we are all guilty of making comparisons. I just wonder at times, though, how those players of the 70s would have fared in the present team. Would Bennett behind the pack that went to Australia have fared any better? What would Gareth Edwards have done with the possession that was so laboured? They should thank their lucky stars that by mere accident their playing careers coincided. They were a joy to watch, and any rugby player would be proud to have been part of it. What I and my contemporaries inherited was the frustration of not being as good or as successful. Incidentally, I don't think the pack of the 70s were given anywhere near as much credit as they deserved. Without them, the stars would have been frustrated extras. Yes, even Bobby Windsor played his part in that dark, twilight world of the front row.

Whereas Wales enjoyed front of stage in the 70s, other countries now seem capable of producing world-quality players on a more regular basis. I've played with and against most of them, and though tempted to nominate a Best of the World XV with the likes of Edwards and Bennett on board, I prefer to base my selection on first-hand knowledge rather than reputation. It might lead to fewer arguments.

Countless hours, I know, are spent naming selections of best fifteens. There's a whole library of such questions available in most pub conversations. Can you pick a team of Welshmen in their positions with fifteen surnames beginning with "W"? Name a team of players with only four letters in their surnames. Pick a team of Welshmen who were born outside Wales (I feature in that one!). The most bizarre is a team of Welshmen who died on active service for their country. I assume that similar questions are asked in the bars of Bath, Beziers and Ballymena.

If only to prove that I would have little merit as a selector, I have scanned the players of my generation and I think those I have chosen would grace any international arena. It is a choice which spans my playing career and though several players enhanced their reputations during the last World Cup, notably the Australians, I was delighted to see that the leading lights did nothing to tarnish reputations.

Naturally I would start with the full-back position, and there is only one contender. The likes of Gavin Hastings of Scotland and John Gallagher of New Zealand are fine individual players. Gavin is particularly strong when coming into the line, and he is the textbook full-back. He's a fearsome spectacle in full flight. I have a great deal of admiration for John Gallagher as well, even more for the players who could create so much space for him for the penetrative runs from the back. The priorities of the position demand a sense of positional play, being able to help your wingers. Dealing with up-and-unders is another priority, and accurate kicking a must. The trouble with playing for Wales is that every kick was vital, since nine times out of ten we were on rearguard action. The pressure of having to get a kick over when the result depends on it is far more intense than being given a kick when your team is fifteen points ahead. That would seem an obvious statement, but it's amazing how many people forget it. Kicking for Wales was always intense! Having listed the qualities of the position I have no hesitation in choosing Serge Blanco as my favourite full-back: a man who had total disregard for the above qualities. But was he a match winner?

To have served France for so long with that exciting sweep of a running action is remarkable in itself. He is vulnerable to the up-and-under but his powers of recovery are amazing. With most full-backs you know exactly what they will do under the high ball, but chasing after Serge Blanco is a different matter. He broke my shoulder, as well; but my man would be Blanco, a rugby entrepreneur and a player who epitomises the French word *charge*. He may have overreacted in the France–England game during the World Cup and it would be a tragedy to have him leave the international scene on a sour note, but for the past decade he has been the very best.

The two wings are also natural choices. I was fortunate enough to play with Stu Wilson once in an invitation fifteen in Ireland and I would love to see more of the Irishman Simon Geoghegan. He certainly tore through our defences on his first visit to the Arms Park. My experience of both, though, is limited. Patrick Lagisquet of France and Trevor Ringland of Ireland were excellent players, a pain in the neck if you know what I mean, and our own Ieuan Evans is a fantastic winger. More's the pity that we could not win enough ball to use him because Ieuan, who doesn't look the athletic type, has a devastating side-step.

No, I have resisted their claims because David Campese of Australia and John Kirwan are world-class in every sense. They have their weaknesses as was seen during the Bledisloe matches of '91, but if you want a sleepless night just think of Kirwan coming at you, ten yards to go and you are the last line of defence. From six foot three, he suddenly becomes eight foot six, and those high-pumping knees look ominously dangerous.

I confess that my appreciation of David Campese owes much to television and of course the World Cup. He was quite exceptional. The Wallabies play such a quick-moving passing game that you don't really recognise what on earth is going on. By watching television you realise how much activity and distraction there is off the ball. One of his tries against Wales during our tour of Australia showed David at his best. The support initiative was bewildering, and even accounting for the poor opposition it was still mesmerising in slow motion. Most people tend to regard him as a winger, but I've seen few people punt the ball as far as Campo from the full-back position. Two match winners in Campese and Kirwan; combined, they would be too much to handle!

On the short list of centres, the likes of England's Jeremy Guscott, the Welshmen John Devereux and Scott Gibbs, Brent Papworth, Tim Horan and Jason Little of Australia give you an indication of the quality of contemporary international rugby. Yet the choice here was easy. The one man to hurt me in a tackle, and I still wince at the easily remembered pain, was Joe Stanley of New Zealand. Here was a play-maker and architect of New Zealand's possession. Grant Fox could concentrate on the basics of punting accuracy, Stanley would be there plotting and orchestrating. He was the man to watch, because Grant offered no threat, since New Zealand rugby uses the outside-half position to extend their options rather than create them. Joe Stanley was so strong and well schooled, like most New Zealanders, in the art of standing in the tackle until the ever-present reinforcements arrived.

Alongside him, and this would be an awesome combination, I would have one of the world's best-ever players. Phillipe Sella of France in my estimation was a very fine player. When he returned to the French team during the World Cup, the attitude of the team was transformed. That is the mark of a great contributor. He came at you so low that it was difficult to position for a tackle, and his strength and determination to get away from any obstruction was never fully appreciated by those who didn't play against him. It would normally take two to stop him, thus creating

110

space for that other nuisance Denis Charvet. Sella has been
a long-time survivor in the French side, and a player who
made me look a bum. Campese, Sella, Stanley and Kirwan:
a few tries among those, I think.

John Rutherford of Scotland was one of my favourite
players. Tall, with silky skills, he had no apparent faults.
Craig Chalmers, who replaced him, has grown into a
confident player. However, in choosing an outside-half I
have looked for the unpredictable. Grant Fox, for all his
points-scoring, is a percentage player and New Zealand's
style of play doesn't place as much emphasis on the position
as we do. Nor does Australia's for that matter, but Michael
Lynagh's contribution cannot be underestimated. His
long-standing partnership with Nick Farr-Jones is a worthy
record, and I didn't fully appreciate how sound a tactician
he was until the Australian tour and his tactical kicking
throughout last October's World Cup. However, if your
pack is that much in command you can drive your team
one-handed.

No, I should want an outside-half who would make the
opposition think and whom they would ignore at their peril.
If I said that he would have to be impish and cheeky, an
improviser and sound in skill, there is only one player who
comes to mind. It was a tragedy that Jonathan Davies went
to the professional code as far as Wales was concerned. Had
he not gone, perhaps a few of the others would have stayed
as well. You never knew what he might do next. If it didn't
come off, something else might. He certainly kept you on
your toes. If he infuriated you, there'd be the sniff of the
nose, a smile, and then he'd depend on instinct for the next
assault. I can just imagine the chat between him and Joe
Stanley! Rugby Union unfortunately didn't see the best of
Jonathan, but Rugby League has.

The scrum-half position beckons so many good players.
Gallion and Berbezier of France, our own Robert Jones, the
World Cup winning captain in '87 David Kirk, Australia's
Nick Farr-Jones and Scotland's Roy Laidlaw and Gary
Armstrong. What an inspiring bunch! They all possess
skills of high quality and brilliant tactical awareness. I have

not included them because my man could, and had to, carry a team – sometimes virtually on his own back.

I am not alone in thinking Terry Holmes to be the best scrum-half ever produced in Wales. Now that should set the tongues wagging! Before anybody mentions Gareth Edwards, I will be the first to express my admiration for Gareth, who was a great player with fantastic skills. Before you throw the book out of the window, let me clarify my thinking. Gareth had a more than reasonable pack in front. Let us not forget their contribution. If the possession wasn't good, he too could look mortal. Though Terry Holmes wasn't given such a cushion, he could, with his immense strength and determination, turn bad possession into attacking platforms. He went looking for trouble, and he was trouble for any back row. He might not have had the best service in the world, perhaps he wasn't the world's most comfortable kicker, but his presence was an inspiration. He carried the Welsh team during his injury-plagued career. To me he was the world's best.

The front row could easily be All Black or All Wallaby. The challenges of Scotland's David Sole and Garuet of France have been noted as well. In that mystical world you almost always have to rely on conversations with other props and hookers. What they do in the tight is alien territory for non-members of the club, but from the full-back position I know whom I loathed meeting in the loose. My choice of hooker is Tommy Lawton of Australia. Has there been a hooker before with his immense size? I know of his mobility because he caught and tackled Serge Blanco once.

His two props are slightly more problematic. Steve McDowell of New Zealand has to go in because I've yet to meet anyone so fit and physical. That front row of New Zealand in the '87 World Cup was an immovable anchor for the All Blacks. Their durability speaks for itself. The same will be said, I have no doubt, of the current Australian front row of McKenzie, Kearns and Daly, but they are still young. My other prop unfortunately went into the professional ranks before maturing into one of the world's best. In so doing he left a huge gap at Neath and in the Welsh camp. Few appreciated Stuart Evans' contribution up front and I've not met many who enjoyed meeting him within the limited confines of front-row battles. I had looked forward to playing under him as captain of Neath, but once again that cheque book did the talking, and away he went. The same happened to David Young, another fine prop who left Wales far too early.

It is a bulky front row, but at the top grade of international rugby, you have to offer more than just size. All three are superb ball handlers and have the speed to match.

I have looked for the same attributes in the rest of the pack and by choosing Gary Whetton of New Zealand and Paul Ackford of England as the two locks, a generous supply of ball is assured, and their dedication to fitness is second to none. The fact that Gary Whetton has survived for so long in the intensity of New Zealand rugby amazes me. To have challenged and taken that grand record of Colin Meads ensures his place with the all-time greats.

There are so many fine locks: Norster of Wales, Steve Cutler of Australia and the newcomers Warwick Waugh and John Eales. And let's not forget Donal Lenihan, Alain Lorieux and Murray Pierce. There's a plentiful supply and I wish a few of them had in recent years found a Welsh grandmother. Paul Ackford, though, is a specialist front-of-the-line jumper and outstanding in the loose. Added to this is his zest for punishing fitness routines, and he more than most has given opposition teams some very worrying afternoons. Despite having some fine players and having regained unity and credibility for me, Paul Ackford stands out as the foundation of the England pack.

Now, if you want a real rugby question, just list the number of quality back-row flankers that have graced the international arenas of the world during the last decade. You'll end up with a rugby telephone directory. So many have excellent and justifiable claims to be included: Winterbottom, Teague, Matthews, Jeffrey, Poidevin, Calder, Whetton, Erbani, Brewer, Carr, Ofanghaue, Champ . . . the list is endless. I wonder why this position more than any other provides so many first-class players?

I have deliberately left my chosen two out of that list.

113

Anyone who has watched international rugby in the last five years will know that the quickest breakaway forward is Michael Jones of New Zealand. Despite his injuries, he has survived and is the spearhead of all New Zealand attacks. His mobility is astonishing and you know that he is never more than a few feet away from the ball. I would have him in any team, except on Sundays. My other choice is less well known and thankfully I have seen little of him myself. During the World XV tour of South Africa we came across a flanker by the name of Vaal Bartmaan. He'll excuse me for saying that he is not the prettiest sight in the world, but all the players recognised in watching Bartmaan play that we'd seen something quite exceptional. Down on the ground, first to the ball, a handler with a turn of speed, it is a tragedy that world rugby has been denied a look at this monster. He'd be in my team, and with Michael Jones alongside I don't think the half-backs would have to worry at all. The opposition half-backs would, though.

I began with an obvious choice at full-back and fortunately, after some soul-searching in other positions, I am confident that most would agree with my choice of no. 8. Despite the claims of Phil Davies of Wales, Dean Richards of England and Australia's Tim Gavin, to me Wayne Shelford of New Zealand reigns supreme. He is a captain who leads by example, a fierce competitor and an explosive player. His athleticism, like that of most of my nominated players, is astonishing, and there are few more terrifying sights on a field than Shelford leading that back row on a charge. How New Zealand missed him in their Bledisloe matches in '91!

So there we have it: Thorburn's World XV. It would have been marvellous to have them together to play a special match of some description. Better still to have them at the Gnoll. I would guarantee a packed house.

WORLD XV

Serge Blanco (France)

John Kirwan (New Zealand)

Phillipe Sella (France)
Joe Stanley (New Zealand)
David Campese (Australia)

Jonathan Davies (Wales)
Terry Holmes (Wales)

Steve McDowell (New Zealand)
Tommy Lawton (Australia)
Stuart Evans (Wales)
Paul Ackford (England)
Garry Whetton (New Zealand)
Vaal Bartmaan (South Africa)
Wayne Shelford (New Zealand)
Michael Jones (New Zealand)

The last decade has been a lean time for Welsh rugby. We have little to show except a Triple Crown under Bleddyn Bowen's captaincy in '88. Tours to Australia and New Zealand, Namibia and Canada have prompted little constructive rebuilding – though perhaps, with the introduction of a technical director and a dozen or so development officers, there is some scope for optimism. I only hope that they are given some visionary targets, or will this new structure too become victim of parochial politics?

If the cupboard has not been laden with victories and trophies, I still believe Wales has produced some fine players during that period. If you don't believe me, ask the scouts with the northern accents.

Seven of my chosen Welsh team followed the now well-trodden route to the grounds of Lancashire and Yorkshire. I do not blame them for seeking financial security, but Wales could not expect to survive such an exit. Neither, for that matter, could any other country.

Jonathan Davies, Terry Holmes, Adrian Hadley, Allan Bateman, Stuart Evans, David Young and Rowland Phillips would feature in my team of the 80s and that is a fair amount of talent. Nearly all were around during the '87 World Cup, and I honestly believe that had we stayed together Welsh rugby would have challenged the best. It takes time to mould a team together, but at one stage it seemed that we were losing a player every week.

The Welsh team I have chosen will cause uproar, if not mirth, in certain quarters. It is not laden with Neath players, as some would expect; but who can deny Neath's contribution to Welsh rugby over the last ten years?

Mike Rayer of Cardiff would be my choice of full-back. Much to his frustration, I'm sure I stayed around a little too long. The Welsh selectors toyed with Anthony Clement in the position, but over the years Mike has shown amazing consistency for his club and has all the hallmarks of a quality full-back. His performance as a replacement in the second World Cup and his game against Argentina showed what an accomplished player he is, and I could not understand why he was dropped for the final match against Australia. There were others, too, who were fine players: Howell Davies of Bridgend, Martin Gravelle of Llanelli, Paul Rees of Cardiff and Mark Wyatt of Swansea, and I'm sure we are going to hear a lot about Luc Evans of Llanelli. But for his sheer consistency of performance over a number of years, Mike Rayer would be my choice.

Ieuan Evans is an automatic choice on one wing and, as I've mentioned, Adrian Hadley would fill the other position. Both players could be match winners, though their styles contrasted. Adrian was particularly difficult to tackle since he was so strong and deceptively fast, whereas Ieuan could combine deception and speed against the best.

Choosing the two centres is more difficult, since Wales has produced quite a few penetrative runners. The unpredictable Mark Ring, the promise of Scott Gibbs and the strength of Robert Ackerman make all three, excellent candidates. However, once again I have been forced to look north for one choice. Welsh rugby did not see the best of Allan Bateman, our centre at Neath. Those who played against him will testify that he was one of the best around, his style of play not dissimilar to Phillipe Sella's. Allan went north and missed the chance of a multitude of caps.

My other centre was one of the most gifted players Wales produced in the 80s. He captained his country to a Triple Crown and was a complete footballer and an instinctive

116

reader of the game. Like so many he was prone to injury, but Bleddyn Bowen in my estimation was one of the best.

The half-backs, again, would be Jonathan and Terry. Behind the scrum Wales would be well equipped to challenge any country. That has been one of the most frustrating facets of my career. We knew we could keep company with most teams, if only we had the ball.

The front row is a difficult area. Brian Williams of Neath would enjoy playing in this side, since parity up front could be achieved, and in that situation there is no finer loose forward. His strength is astonishing and there is no better sight than to see Brian rip the ball away from the maul and charge upfield. A naturally fit player, others found him difficult to cope with because of his speed in the loose. When capped he would lead a charge only to leave others in his wake.

I have not forgotten David Young, but he was so young when he decided to leave the Union game, I don't think we saw his full range of ability. Doubtless he was one of the major successes of the Lions tour of Australia; but I honestly believe that Brian Williams would be an immense player given good company. Stuart Evans stayed around long enough to establish his credentials and his bulk, and I would have no hesitation in wanting him around.

The choice of hooker will raise an eyebrow or two and cause a few glasses to fall. During the past ten years Wales have been served by excellent hookers. Alan Phillips of Cardiff and Billy James of Swansea vied for the slot for years and both had immense skill though they were totally different players: Alan with his eye for an opening and a sprint, Billy content to concentrate in the tight and on the fringes.

Along came Ian Watkins, who but for injury would have probably seen off other challenges. To my mind, though, Kevin Phillips, often criticised for his throwing-in at the line-out, had exceptional skills as a mobile hooker. Not only that: there have been few better motivators at the Gnoll or even at the Arms Park. He has his critics, I'm aware of that, but he's the man I'd want in my team to inspire those around him.

Yes, I am aware that I have selected an all-Neath front row. I will stand accused of bias, but that front row would match any other Welsh selection. It annoys me that we didn't see the best of Brian Williams because the support wasn't present, and the splendid encouragement of Kevin Phillips would only be appreciated by those who were there. I plead guilty therefore to all charges.

In the second row, Robert Norster and Richard Moriarty are automatic choices. At the beginning of this chapter I bemoaned the lack of big, robust men in Wales. Both Robert and Richard are not only big but they are also mobile. On his day, there was no finer line-out jumper in the world than Robert, and I always remember his superb timing in South Africa before being injured. Richard Moriarty, too, excelled in the line-out but could also motivate his fellow players by leading from the front. Sadly, both players were plagued by injury. When fully fit they were excellent.

As in the World XV, the back row presents a multitude of problems. I haven't counted how many back-row players have been selected for Wales in the 80s, but it's not an area where we are short of quality players. Emyr Lewis of Llanelli will, I believe, become one of the best around. He at least in Australia could hold his head high and was one of the few to reach anything like his potential in the World Cup. There have been so many others, too: Martyn Morris, Paul Moriarty, David Pickering and Richie Collins.

On the blind side I have played with no harder man than Phil Pugh. He has that single-minded approach to the game that sometimes gets him into trouble, but on his day there was no finer exponent of damaging the opposition rhythm. He would be a must for me.

At open side we have a store of contenders. Richard Webster's time will come again, I'm sure, because he too has that determination which never flinches. Yet for me, the one man capable of getting amongst the opposition and with a massive appetite for work was Gareth Roberts, now with Cardiff. There were some who were reluctant to become involved in the fray; not Gareth, who often spent more time at the bottom of a ruck than outside it.

118

At no. 8 many would expect me to opt for Phil Davies. He is a trojan, and when fully fit could single-handed lift the Welsh team's morale on his own. Perhaps he wasn't as mobile as other no. 8s and I have always harboured a thought that his best position might have been in the front row.

At no. 8 for me would be another of the game's defectors. Rowland Phillips (yes I know he played for Neath) was a marvellous player to have alongside. Of all the players at the Gnoll who departed for the professional game, Rowland was the greatest loss. He was fantastically strong on the drive, had the ability to handle well and covered an enormous amount of territory. He's my man, and that is my team.

WALES XV

Michael Rayer (Cardiff)

Ieuan Evans (Llanelli)
Allan Bateman (Neath)
Bleddyn Bowen (Swansea)
Adrian Hadley (Cardiff)

Jonathan Davies (Llanelli)
Terry Holmes (Cardiff)

Brian Williams (Neath)
Kevin Phillips (Neath)
Stuart Evans (Neath)
Robert Norster (Cardiff)
Richard Moriarty (Swansea)
Phil Pugh (Neath)
Rowland Phillips (Neath)
Gareth Roberts (Cardiff)

9

An International Season for Wales '91

Success may well have been the keyword for Welsh rugby in the 70s. It is little wonder that so many of those great names were not attracted by the temptation of Rugby League. They had no need to seek greener pastures, nor were they castigated by the poisonous pens, or at least, not to the same degree as at present. They were, to all intents, a talented collection of individuals who played like a club team, and a vast number of them were automatic choices. Why should they have been lured to the anonymity of the north when they were embraced by so much goodwill in the south? A few defected, but have returned.

The men of the 70s were special. Not many selections have prompted such an outcry as when Phil Bennett was demoted from the national side, since tampering with success was tantamount to treason. Watching from a distance at Hereford Cathedral School was one P. Thorburn. They were heroes, torchbearers and players to emulate.

By the late 80s, the climate had changed. The Rugby League scouts followed the southbound motorways, and after secretive meetings in Worcester hotels picked the best of our bunch. I doubt that there is a single rugby-playing country in the world which could have survived such trawl of talent. So, whereas success was the norm of the 70s, survival was uppermost in my mind during the late 80s and early 90s. To be realistic, sometimes we achieved moderate success against Five Nations teams, but against that other lot from Down Under, we had no chance at all.

The '91 Five Nations campaign for Wales epitomised all we had to endure in an international season. Having returned from Namibia during the summer months, we concentrated all our thoughts on building a team worthy of a proud nation. It wasn't going to be easy after the whitewash of the previous campaign. We were going to begin at the bottom, and there was only one way to go.

There was the matter of meeting the Barbarians, first of all. The WRU had somewhat controversially decided to award full caps for the match. Whether they were right or wrong in doing so is not my concern, because once the red jersey was on my back, motivation was not a problem. During the Namibian tour, as well, many scoffed at the thought of full caps against the world's youngest rugby nation. I suppose it all harks back to the traditionalists of the East India Club who would want the IRB membership board defended against all erosion. Yet it doesn't make sense to award caps during the World Cup against the likes of Tonga, Western Samoa or Zimbabwe, if you are not going to honour those countries with the same respect on tours.

The Welsh match against the Barbarians was a bit of a curate's egg. I kicked well enough, scored a try and gave one away. The Barbarians had only narrowly lost to England, and we knew that it was not going to be an exhibition afternoon. Mark Jones did his usual by conceding a daft penalty, and we struggled from there on. It was another defeat for Wales, fodder for the critics, and I'd met the quickest flanker I'd seen on two feet, an uncapped New Zealander called Eric Rush – the man who charged down my kick and won the game. The scribes began predicting our downfall against England at Cardiff in January before we had reached the changing room. The campaign was on. It began disastrously.

Mark Jones went north, and Martyn Morris was sent off in a Neath game against Newport, a game in which we lost our unbeaten club record. I was away in Ireland at the time with Ann's family, so fortunately I could avoid the inevitable chuckles of the anti-Neath brigade. Ann and Kelly stayed in Ireland, which was just as well, because the date – 19 January, Wales v. England – was firmly implanted by now and the sleepless nights had begun. We had no back row. No one could predict the composition of the front row with any confidence, and Wales were now without the retired Bob Norster. I was lucky to sleep at all.

I've heard the wisecracks about my being too hyped up for a game before, and no doubt I'll hear them again. "Imagine a Welsh captain crying before a game," said one eminent senior rugby journalist, "it's preposterous." Yet for three weeks before the England game, there was constant reference to the fact that Wales had not been beaten at Cardiff by England for twenty-eight years. Was I going to be the captain to surrender that record? Clive Rowlands, the last losing Welsh captain in 1963, told me that he had dined on that distinction for a quarter of a century. It was a typical Clive remark. A quip, a smile and a glance to note the reaction. I didn't want any such invitations, and the pressure began.

Hardly a newspaper was published without some reference to that day when the braziers were on the field and Malcolm Phillips scored the winning try. We knew that England would come to Cardiff with confidence after the hiding we'd received at Twickenham the year before. Naturally, the England press began predicting outrageous scores, which I imagine brought extra pressure to bear on the captain, Will Carling. That was his bad fortune; I had enough to think about.

Ron Waldron recognised what might be going through the players' minds, so he organised a Saturday night thrash at the Holiday Inn in Cardiff a fortnight before the England match. It was a splendid gesture, enjoyed by all except the banned Martyn Morris and Richard Webster, who had broken his hand playing for Swansea. The players' wives were there except for Ann, but whenever you got into a discussion, that game, only a fortnight away, was an ever-present topic of conversation.

God, it was like a war! To read the likes of John Reason, you would think that the whole of Wales would disappear if they lost to England. I suppose he was right in one respect, as for many it was that important. You were expected to die for the cause; yet how could I die a happy man knowing that I'd been captain of a losing side against England at Cardiff?

The next morning we were called to a squad training session. It was a rather frightening experience, since there were so many unfamiliar faces. I didn't doubt the ability of the players involved in that session, but here we were within a few days of meeting a confident England team, and I wasn't on first-name terms with some of the players! It must have been quite something back in the 70s to turn up for a session with the likes of J.P.R., Gareth Edwards, Dai Morris, Phil Bennett, and so on. They probably knew each other as well as they knew their wives! It was so different twenty years on, and to my eternal regret to have some of those to join in the clamour did nothing for the team morale. How would Gareth or Phil have fared behind the young Welsh pack of the late 80s and 90s?

That week, Adrian Davies made himself unavailable because of Cambridge commitments and Andrew Kembury went down with a hairline fracture of his cheekbone. Ieuan Evans declared himself fit and then promptly pulled a hamstring. Not bad going so far!

The team announcement was made to the players ten days before the match. It is always unnerving, because until that announcement is made, there is no security. Ex-internationals have always complained about not being told when they were dropped, and to receive an explanation as to your dismissal would require a papal edict. They will be comforted to know that by and large the system hasn't changed. The disgusting lack of courtesy has become a norm, but then the conversations I've heard from committeemen about selectors, coaches and any other non-elected positions has made me glad I'm a player.

There was a press conference at the end of the announcement, and all the squad were present for interviews and photographs. That was a splendid move, since from that moment on, the whole world would want to speak to the players concerned, and of course the subject would be that bloody record.

Considering the defections and the injuries, we were lucky to muster a team. For personal reasons, Phil Davies wasn't available for international selection. The speculation in the press about his weight did him no favours and it was a badly-kept secret that Ron didn't think the Llanelli trojan was fit enough to play international rugby. Phil withdrew behind a wall of silence, biding his time. Glen George and Alun Carter of Newport, who were reported to have excelled in a game against Neath, were called into the team and Neil Jenkins the Pontypridd outside-half and our own Scott Gibbs were also going to make their débuts. I retained the captaincy from the Barbarians match, but knew that with such inexperience we were going to struggle, especially up front.

Apart from building up steam for this clash, there were other matters to attend to. Neath lost their ground record to Llanelli, and, ominously for the Welsh selectors, the back row of Phil Davies, Emyr Lewis and Lyn Jones saw us off the park.

As the Welsh players' representative on the amateur regulations committee, I was asked to meet representatives of First Artists Corporation. They had been appointed as agents to the Welsh squad by the Union. I listened as they spoke of gathering £200,000 for the squad through various forms of sponsorship. It was impressive, but I remember thinking that for all the promises, it sounded like good selling banter with no real substance. Anyway, if the regulations had been relaxed, why wasn't something in place before now, and not a few days before the Five Nations biggest match of the season for Wales? It seemed so late to be reacting, but at least it was something. The message from the marketing boys was clear. The more successful we were to be, the more marketable we would become. I did at that time wonder if we had enough dedication within the team to realise our potential, not only on the field, but off it as well. It was all well and good to be talking about pots of gold, but I knew as a member of that Committee that unless certain players changed their attitudes the dirty streets of Cardiff would never be paved with gold.

In all honesty I admired the way the marketeers smiled as they spoke of "attainable" targets and endorsements. It was another world, but if we were ever to reach that threshold there was an awful lot to be done by ourselves. It was no use complaining that players in other parts of the world were raking it in, and we had been left as the rugby paupers of the globe. We had achieved nothing, were not likely to achieve anything, because we simply were not working hard enough.

When the Union appointed Jonathan Price as its commercial director, he was presented to us by Ron Waldron. I don't care if Tony O'Reilly had been appointed. It wouldn't have mattered. The players seemed to think that merely because the WRU had now brought in a commercial man to look after the union's affairs, the contracts would come flying in. The real world was, and is, a harsh one. The reality was that a losing team and the fractured state of Welsh rugby was nigh unmarketable. Whatever came, if anything, would be a bonus.

After the Llanelli defeat, I spent Sunday in a mood of depression and emptiness. The clouds were gathering and I recognised that P. Thorburn was not in a positive frame of mind at all. There were a few days to go before the England match and the demands would allow little time for personal motivation. A BBC show had to be recorded with Roy Noble, a £360,000 cheque had to be presented to a pools winner and there was another presentation to be re-arranged. All this on top of my work with Westdale Press and the nine follow-up calls to be done on Tuesday alone! The pools winner said the money wouldn't change his life, so I suggested he hand over the cheque to me.

Ironically, before handing over that cheque, I was enlightened as to what a marketable product a rugby player could be. I had accepted a nominal fee for turning up for the presentation, but the hard-bitten journalists at Rugby Vision Ltd, a favourite coffee stop of mine, told me what a naive fool I was to be so charitable to a multi-million pound organisation. I left Rugby Vision, phoned up my contact, trebled the fee and realised that I needed an agent or counsel. That meant another cup of coffee at Rugby Vision Ltd the next morning.

The late Tuesday evening training session went well enough, with most of us realising that if we concentrated for eighty minutes we could do it. I had the words of the National Anthem printed so the boys could at least mumble correctly. The cameras always go along the teams when the Anthem is played and there is nothing worse than a blank, frowning stare at the committee box when the band (inevitably out of sync with the rest of us) is blasting away. Some of the boys thought this a bit peculiar. After all, why should a Welsh player born in Germany and educated in England be so concerned with the words of "Hen Wlad Fy Nhadau"? My answer to that was "Have you seen the All Blacks not throw everything they have into the Haka?"

Neil Jenkins, the new outside-half, looked confident at the run-out. My hope was that he would show the same attitude against Peter Winterbottom.

On the Friday, when we gathered at the Angel Hotel after a light training session, the mood of the team was fairly confident, especially that of the newcomers. However, personally, the weight on me was unbearable. I felt like an old man. I was in that irritable, snappy sort of mood. The family and close friends recognise the mood and give me a wide berth. It is a state of mind. The supporters, the press, the bulletins and the stupid comments from people who should know better got to me . . . I just wondered whether it was worth it.

I won the toss and chose to play into the wind and sun, hoping that the low sun over the Arms Park stands would give Simon Hodgkinson a difficult time in the second half. The clouds wrecked my plans.

We started well enough and placed England under enough pressure for them to concede a penalty. From that moment on I had a nightmare. Of all the days for my kicking to go to pieces, I had to pick this one. I simply could not put a foot right, and to this day I cannot explain why I should look a dummy, while Simon Hodgkinson slotted everything he could. My head went down. I had let my country down, and I had failed to convert pressure into points. Who can explain a sudden loss of form? I would willingly have exchanged my kicks against the Barbarians for a few successful ones against England. I was going to be the captain of the first losing side against England for twenty-eight years. Something to tell my grandchildren, because if I didn't, someone else would!

I was devastated. So too were the crowd. I was not to be forgiven, and my brother in the crowd heard so much abuse that he vowed never to watch me play again. He phoned me later in the week to say that he couldn't take any more; he couldn't understand the East versus West divide in Wales.

The feeling of numbness was overwhelming, and had it not been for the attitude of the England players in their much publicised "no comment" war with the television and press boys, it would have been much worse. Will Carling and the England team had collectively decided to ignore the media. For whatever reason, I was grateful, because it deflected much of the attention from our demise and indeed England's achievement, to the annoyance of the press gang not being able to scribble their quotes. Even they had waited a long time for this moment and to be told that they were not going to get their quotes had them boiling for days.

As a player, I couldn't help smiling a little a few days after the event. There is nothing more indignant than some of the media when they are denied their so-called right of free speech. I just wish they would quote correctly when they are told something. Will Carling that evening, sitting alongside me, was not the picture of a victorious captain, the first in Cardiff for twenty-eight years. The Twickenham establishment had got to him, and he'd been told in no uncertain terms what they thought of the media "gag". Then the irony struck me. Whereas I had been castigated for shooting my mouth off, here was the England captain being pilloried for sending the press to Coventry.

The after-match function was a rather shambolic affair. Profiteroles became flying saucers and not too many brain cells were functioning the next morning, especially in West Wales!

127

On the Sunday morning, because I knew that the depression would really get a hold of me in that little world or domain where perspective is absent, I decided to retire. It was not encouraging, either, to hear the family report some of the comments from the terraces. You wonder sometimes if a few of them are worthy of red scarves and hats. I didn't want the family to watch any longer, because apart from any other consideration, I know how "involved" they could get if I was the subject of abuse. A few supporters around the country will testify to that.

I couldn't face work on Monday, either, though I have to say the people at Westdale Press had always been support-ive. I knew though, that what was left unsaid would be thought, and that was probably worse. Emotionally drained and a physical wreck, I went to bed at eight that evening, opting out of club training, which was the last thing I wanted to face.

Rationalisation took over. There had been good times, and they should be placed alongside what I was now going through. Eventually the clouds lifted, and believe it or not, there were a few encouraging comments to be found in the columns. More importantly, Neath were due to play Newport in a Schweppes Cup match on Saturday. There was no rest, no time for reflection, and that is why I didn't pack up international rugby that week. The temptations had been there, but the Welsh rugby timetable, that devourer of mental and physical strength, took over once again.

As I approached the Gnoll for that match, a young Newport supporter came up to me and said, "Hope you kick as badly today as you did last week." He was offered a few compliments of the season, but at least with a wry smile.

The match against Newport was predictably hard and physical, as taxing as any international. Phil Pugh was sent off, which inevitably attracted the headlines, but it was one of those games that you have to endure and survive. The relief of winning and forcing Newport to concede two penalty tries through collapsed scrums was thoroughly satisfying. But the toll on my physical condition was heavy.

128

The lads from other countries, especially Ireland and Scotland always comment on the emotional ferocity of the Welsh games they watch on Sunday afternoons. Every contest, especially at the Gnoll, is a combative experience watched by fanatics and played by those who will not settle for second best. All this between internationals.

The Welsh team to travel to Scotland had been announced and it was comforting to have an unchanged side. There had been a few pluses in the England match, notably our scrummaging, and the old warhorse, Charlie Faulkner, drafted in for his expertise, had been pleased with that facet of our game.

For every international there is a personal timetable. It isn't one that you schedule yourself; it just has a habit of being dictated by events. By the Wednesday before a game, thoughts are of little else. All the humdrum domesticities float by and comments made by well-wishers don't really register. It is as if you are on another plane of operation. I confess that I do get short-fused and easily provoked. It happened on this occasion when the Welsh team were training in Cardiff before departing for Edinburgh. The practice ground was covered with snow and Robert Jones, David Evans and Mark Ring began the inevitable snowball fight. I lost my cool in the freezing temperatures and gave them a sharp rebuke. I sometimes wonder what they think of me? Am I too uptight? But then I don't appreciate any larking about in training, especially at international level. Have your lark-about when the job is done!

After a delay at Cardiff Airport, we eventually arrived in Scotland. The Welsh supporters, also frustrated by delayed flights, knew only too well how to spend the waiting hours. One of these days, I told myself, I'll be there with you. Can't really wait for the days when you can let go.

There are three memories of the days and hours before the Murrayfield match. One was the conversation about AIDS with the Newbridge hooker, Kenny Waters, as we were walking up Princes Street. After the walk, Kenny picked up a flu bug, so that will teach us to go wandering into the Edinburgh night. The second was Paul Burnell's comments about the Neath boys in the Welsh team. The

Scots prop had a go at the Neath haircuts, castigating them for the way they looked and questioning how on earth such a bunch of renegades could represent their country. Those comments went down well, I can tell you! The last was the result of Neath's match with London Scottish. Neath had been hammered.

On the Friday, I practised my kicking and was not so confident. For some reason, I was hooking again. And that was not good. Nor was the Saturday morning walk along Princes Street – the traditional way of waking up and meeting half the Welsh male population. I stepped out of a sports shop after buying a pair of shorts.

"Been in to buy a pair of boots have you?" said this half-cut Welsh "supporter".

"No," I replied. "Why should I?"

" 'Cos you bloody well need them!" he shouted.

That really generated confidence. At least we had remembered how cold it could be in Scotland before the match. As is the custom these days, Scotland's Number One fan was to be introduced to us and we waited for Her Royal Highness The Princess Royal in tracksuits. Previously it had been a wait in the freezing temperatures, which isn't the best way of starting a match against the men in blue. I wonder, now that the Princess of Wales has honoured Wales with a visit to the Arms Park during the World Cup, whether our lads will enjoy the same regular patronage.

I don't know whether it was the length of the formalities or the singing of "Flower of Scotland", but we began as if we'd just got off the plane. Scotland tore our so-called improved scrummaging apart, and we never recovered. On the limited possession we had, our backs did well enough and carved out a good try for Steve Ford. I felt a little happier with my game, but in the end after the inspirational arrival of Kenny Milne on the field, Scotland had us by the jugular. Mind you, I have to say this: the Scots are the masters of taking men out. I only wish there was some consistency in refereeing, but time and again the Scots back row would break, blocking a channel for the ball carrier. According to the laws of the game that should be illegal, but if the referee allows such obstruction, you shouldn't complain – but I just have. It is a point for future referees of the Scots, because the players are too canny to take any notice of a losing captain's whingeing. Once again, I resigned myself to a week of recrimination and criticism. It wasn't as bad as some of the others.

I had left the field ten minutes before the end with a bruised ankle which required an X-ray at a local hospital. After I returned to the team hotel, there were few happy faces. Ron Waldron was obviously disappointed, not only with the result, a 32–12 defeat, but with our overall performance, especially in the scrummaging department. He knew that that hammering inflicted upon our front row would be small fry compared with the bludgeons being swung by the media. Brian Williams was devastated and knew that his career as an international prop was over. In tears he talked all the time of retirement. It was a tragedy because in a winning pack he is one of the finest forwards of all time. A stronger man you will not find, and he'll give you everything until the final whistle.

We waited for the brickbats, and they were not long in coming. "How long are we as a nation going to put up with this?" wrote Clem Thomas. The venom factory went into overdrive, and few came out unscathed apart from young Scott Gibbs, who was having a marvellous introduction to international rugby.

We knew there were bound to be major changes for our next game against Ireland, and we were not disappointed. For Ron to have continued his selection policy on mobility alone would have been suicidal. Whereas it had worked so emphatically at Neath, the demands at international level had been that much greater. Somewhere some big men had to be found to compete for possession. Out went Brian Williams, Paul Knight, Glen George and Alun Carter and in came Mike Griffiths, John Davies, Phil Davies and Martyn Morris. It was a mixture of delight and sadness for me. I was delighted for John, another Pembrokeshire farmer to be gaining his first cap, yet sorry that his father wasn't there to see it: he'd died a few months before. I felt sadness for Brian, and sympathy too for Robert Jones who had also been dropped.

Robert felt so indignant about his treatment that he had

a go at Ron through the Welsh newspaper columns. To a certain degree I could understand his frustration, but at Swansea and for Wales he'd been unable to display his full arsenal behind a beaten pack. Given a platform, he ranks with the world's best. I don't think it helped his cause to have gone to the press so readily, but he was a bitter man. He should have waited, biding his time to make a point or two when given the opportunity.

It was already being dubbed the match of the also-rans by the press, or the second division championship. I doubt whether the Irish players appreciated that; I know we didn't. Whatever has happened in previous matches, it's amazing how the mind concentrates on the immediate future. The task was quite simply a quest for credibility and survival. I kept telling myself, "We've got to win some bloody time." The desire to win, just to relieve the pressure valve a little, was enormous.

I was happy to have Phil Davies back in the team. Privately, he'd been like a raging bull wanting to get back into the international arena. "I've got to get back in," he told me. "I've been out long enough." He is an awesome sight for opponents, as I know only too well, and an excellent player. It was good too to have Martyn Morris recognised for the amazing, destructive speed he has around the field.

Ireland, too, had made a few changes, all behind the scrum, and had left out Michael Kiernan: this hadn't been a popular move, according to the Irish press. The message to be driven home was that we badly needed possession to release our threequarters.

The match began well with some fine drives, and the Arms Park crowd, knowing how desperate we were for success, were right behind us. As has happened so often against the Irish, it was whirlwind stuff, incredibly fast and patternless. The drives were good, and we should have made more use behind of the forward effort. The Irish backs were well aware of our intentions and disrupted the Welsh threequarters with some characteristic Celtic charges. Brendan Mullin got hold of Scott early on and gave him one of those "glad to know you tackles", and we lost our rhythm. They got amongst us and our lines of alignment were in a bit of a mess. There was also one Simon Geoghegan on the right wing to deal with since he'd already turned us once or twice. He was proving to be quite a handful for Steve Ford and despite a try by Paul Arnold and a few kicks of mine, we had a workable lead. Yet it was that kind of game, and despite all the concentration I could muster in that hectic cauldron, I missed a vital tackle; that was enough for Ireland to recharge the limbs. As soon as I'd missed the tackle, I knew that volumes would be written about another weakness in my game. I made a mental note to pump more iron and tried desperately to get the boys to hang in there.

Back came Geoghegan and the Irish and we settled for a draw. It shouldn't have been on level terms. I had missed that crucial tackle, Mark Ring had a kick charged down which ended up as an Irish score; but the early pressure had not been enough. Despite the result, it was one of the most enjoyable games that I have played in at international level. It was mayhem, it was frantic, but it was an enjoyable game. More's the pity that we couldn't have recorded a win, since there had been a few encouraging signs from the pack. At least at 21–21 I would not end up as captain of a whitewash season. It was small consolation – but, believe me, it was a relief.

After the match there was the usual round of interviews and having to face the press. I suppose the Welsh scribes had already written us off since I don't recall any hard questioning. Yet when it came to the turn of the Irish selectors to be questioned, the Irish press let rip. The non-selection of Michael Kiernan as a reliable points scorer had mystified the Irish rugby press for a week. Brian Smith had not had a good afternoon and the Irish journalists were going to have a real go at the Irish coach for such a cock-up in selection. I challenged the questioner, who was not, I think, a journalist, by telling him that Brian Smith was one of the finest kickers around and that people in the stand didn't realise how difficult it was to get the measure of the Arms Park wind and its sudden swirling changes.

We had a good night with the Irish in Cardiff, as had

been the custom over the years. Will Carling, the England captain, has written that he wouldn't fancy having a pint with the Welsh boys after an international; but the Irish, I suppose, are closer to the Welsh than the St George's Channel might suggest, and once the final whistle has blown, anything goes. Unfortunately, the Welsh press seemed to think that it was too good a night, and suggested that the team was not disappointed enough in defeat. It was absolute rubbish, and yet again I was amazed at how crass and stupid some of them can be. If a journalist seriously thought that we enjoyed being defeated, actually couldn't care tuppence about being the basement boys of the Five Nations . . . but then they have to write something!

Mark Ring was in tears that night, while others opted for other ways of getting rid of their frustration. That is their choice. Personally, I knew that there was another mountain on the horizon. As the seasonal calendar would have it, there was one to go. The last match of the season was against France at Parc des Princes, the Gallic fortress where Wales hadn't won since 1975, let alone the fact that we hadn't beaten the French in ten years. My only message to the players was "Of all the games you'll ever play in, this will be the most difficult. We will have to get between them and turn them around." Grand words, but how the hell were we going to do it?

I told the television and press interviewers that I was optimistic after encouraging signs against Scotland and Ireland, but personally I knew we'd be lucky to come second. Facing the French at Cardiff was bad enough, but I knew what a taxing afternoon it would be for the youngsters in the team when they ran out on to Parc des Princes. Internationals from other countries have claimed that they find the Arms Park and its crowd intimidating. I hope so. Equally, the French crowd right on top of you, with the incredible noise they generate, is nerve-tingling. If you allow the French an inch, or a few points' lead, that noise will stay with you for the rest of your life. It has always seemed to be a faster game in Paris as well. Maybe it's the close-cropped grass which feels like a running track, but I swear that matches at Parc des Princes are a yard faster.

I had stressed to the team how important the game was, so I was annoyed to see some of them clowning around at training. So much of international rugby is about attitude and if that isn't totally concentrated on the matter at hand then you might as well quit. Perhaps the papers had got to some of them. No one gave us a flicker of hope. We were the dregs of the Five Nations and no public utterances of optimism were going to alter one word written by the prophets of doom. They were right of course, I knew that, but what I had hoped was that the resolve of the lads would be stiffened. Serge Blanco had announced that it was going to be his last game in the Five Nations Championship at Parc des Princes and I was delighted to be part of a rather special game.

Once the game began, inevitably at a furious pace, our forwards did well enough to hold their own, and that was a tremendous achievement. It was the backs who completely froze this time, with the angles haphazard and the occasion proving too much for them. Serge once again scored his customary try, following one of our high up-and-under kicks, and at half-time we were down 16–3. I have to confess that it was an enjoyable match to watch, so fast and furious and superbly constructed by the French. Our heads had gone down, the fight had gone and another heavy defeat loomed. There was little to be done about it. No use crying now. The speeches about letting down your family, brothers, sisters, cousins and friends matter little when your back is eternally stuck to the wall.

The after-match function was a tribute to Serge Blanco, an amazing player who has withstood the challenge of time. I wish I had been down on the tables with the boys. Top table was no place to be at the end of another thoroughly disappointing season with only a few words of French. Serge was fêted since he'd calculated so perfectly the timing of his retirement. That was his last game in the Five Nations; his last for France would be in the World Cup.

He said farewell. I wish I could have done the same.

10

Down (Under) and Out

On my arrival home from the Welsh tour of Australia, Ann had pranged the car into a wall at the Arms Park. Despite the damage to the front fender, I couldn't have cared less. I was just glad to see her and Kelly. The relief was enormous, and I realised that my priorities had got a little out of hand.

The tour had been an enormous strain. I wanted to unburden myself of the guilt feelings, the worries and the anger that I felt towards certain individuals. I was conscious of the '91 Rugby World Cup around the corner and of a match against France to celebrate the opening of the Arms Park lights. It would be the same intensity without respite. Life, or ordinary life, and an individual's emotions, would become secondary to the hourly demands of other people.

I wanted out. The brain, or what was left of it, couldn't take any more punishment. I also knew that Ron was on his way out. The strain had got to him as well. No one who hasn't experienced that almost monastic self-examination will ever know the despair of failure. At that time if someone had told me that I wouldn't see another rugby ball for the rest of my life, it wouldn't have mattered.

After my return I was asked to attend a briefing on the tour by Denis Evans, the Welsh Rugby Union secretary. I told him the lot, because I had already poured out my feelings to Clive Rowlands, the tour manager. That was a meeting I would rather forget. It was before the test match against Australia, and I broke down in front of Clive in his hotel bedroom. The Welsh tour had been a colossal disaster, not because of the results, nor because of Ron, but because of the players' attitude towards the management and the lack of respect they had for themselves. Some of them should never have been there, in my view. The subsequent pruning of the Welsh squad for the World Cup went some way to convince me that I hadn't gone absolutely crackers.

Although I had made up my mind to retire before I had the meeting with Denis, I suppose the exercise concentrated my mind on all the ills that had befallen Welsh rugby. Throughout I had consulted Ann, who wasn't entirely in agreement with my decision, but as ever, very supportive. I consulted a few friends as to the best course of action, and they all questioned the wisdom of retiring at that particular time. However, my decision was final. A letter was sent to the Union on Saturday 2 August.

Dear Denis,

It is with regret and sadness that I write to inform you that I have decided that I no longer wish to be considered for Wales.

Prior to the test match against Australia, I informed Clive Rowlands, the team manager, of my intentions and so hopefully my decision will not come as a complete shock to you.

Sadly, as we discussed over lunch last week, I felt strongly about the attitudes of certain members of the touring party and felt at the time, as indeed I still feel, that the approach by many is not one which will see Welsh rugby reach the top.

My action I know comes at a time when Wales really needs all the help it can get, but I feel so strongly about certain events that my decision is final.

I did stress my feeling to you at that lunch and have felt for a number of years that there were problems relating to players' attitudes, especially off the field. The remarks certain players made about Ron and the general coaching were widespread, yet not one player commented on the lack of effort in training especially prior to the tour.

Over the last three years, members of the squad have been given advice on both fitness and dietary controls specifically for sportsmen, and it is blatantly obvious that only some of the squad religiously adhered to those schedules.

I certainly do not consider myself to be perfect as I know there are many weaknesses in my game and I have made many mistakes over the years, but I certainly work hard in attempting to rectify these problems. Sadly, this effort is not widespread amongst the squad.

I do not envy you or anyone else in the Union with the task ahead but would like to pass on my sincere thanks to everybody I have had association with over the last six or seven years. I have thoroughly enjoyed my time on the international scene and for that my thanks go to you and your colleagues.

Finally, I would like to offer my apologies for any inconvenience I have caused the Union as a result of my actions over the last few years; sadly, the pressures have now become too great for me to handle.

I would like to wish those in Welsh rugby who deserve success every bit of luck in the future and I will always be proud to have been part of the Welsh international rugby scene.

Yours sincerely,
Paul Thorburn

Denis Evans in reply through press quotes the next day said he wasn't surprised to receive my letter. Forty-eight hours before being informed of my decision, he had held a strongly worded press conference to express his anger at the behaviour of the Welsh party in Australia, a party which incidentally included two WRU Presidents, a manager and coach and two selectors. Discipline should not have been a problem. But it was.

My resignation was welcomed in some quarters, as I knew it would be. The story appeared in the *Sunday People* with a few chosen quotes under the headline "I quit". My initial article for the paper was strongly worded because I wanted to tell the truth, or at least tell how I had witnessed certain incidents in Australia. However, my father, after reading a draft of the article, blew his top and demanded that I seek a retraction. The argument raged between father and son, and eventually, through some delicate negotiations, I managed to persuade the paper to print a watered-down version. They were none too pleased, nor were those negotiating on my behalf, but peace was restored in the Thorburn household, until the next episode.

Once the article had appeared and the letter had been delivered, we spent the Sunday hiding away under the shadow of Carreg Cennen, a magnificent Celtic castle in the Towy Valley.

My father was naturally disappointed with my decision but if I was to go, then it had to be done with some dignity. There was little point, he argued, in castigating certain players: there was no dignity in that. Yet, at the back of my mind, I knew that it was their behaviour that had been instrumental in my decision.

The local coverage was intense, and somehow or other a few "touring" stories began to emerge. It was said that I had come to blows with the Pontypridd centre, Steele Lewis, and that Mike Griffiths, the international prop, had spat in my face on the homeward journey. Both demanded that the Union clear their names from these allegations; an investigation was launched but nothing came of it. It didn't help matters that a forty-seven man Welsh squad had just been announced for the World Cup season with Steele Lewis left out. It added fuel to the row, since it appeared that he was being disciplined. The truth of the matter was, according to one of our touring selectors, that he lacked genuine pace and had apparently been beaten in the sprints by one of the management.

On television I made the point that both stories were very much exaggerated. It was true that Steele and I had had words one night, I in defence of Ron Waldron and his coaching methods. Steele wanted to put the blame for the lack of Welsh success entirely at Ron's door. I wouldn't have that and, to avoid further unpleasantness, I left. The next morning, as so often happens on tours, the incident was forgotten.

If the Australian Rugby Union should ever decide not to invite Wales to tour again, I would understand. We were a bunch of whingers and drinkers. I have no regrets about telling the truth, because the time has come for Welsh rugby players, if they want to compete with the world's best, to be honest with themselves. A player who drinks himself into a stupor on the homeward flight has no place in the modern rugby arena, in my opinion. An international who doesn't care enough about his own pride, and resorts to insulting the Welsh national coach, has no place in international rugby. I also believe that to cause a fracas, whatever the cause, before an invited audience, including the world rugby press, is inexcusable. I am no saint and I knew on at least one occasion when I blew my top, I let myself and the boys down. However, I cannot understand how Welsh players with continual hangovers can expect to compete with the Australians and New Zealanders of this world. It is perhaps not a reflection of their own lack of self-discipline but of that prevailing in their clubs.

For some of our senior players, seasoned internationals, not to give of their best, preferring the wine bottle to the training ground, is inexplicable. For some of my own club players from Neath to square up to fellow Welsh squad members, hoping to be recognised as the "hard men" of the tour, was pathetic. To make mockery of the management merely underlined the fact that a number of players were so totally immature that they would have been better left at home. That is what I believe.

No management team is faultless, nor would successful ones claim to be. To achieve success, managers at all levels have to learn from their mistakes. I have never entirely agreed with Ron Waldron's methods, but I have always had enormous respect for him. I would respect any national coach of Wales and keep counsel with myself if in doubt about decisions and tactics. Not some of our touring party. They knew better, and in the dark corners of the Australian wine bars, there was little talk of supporting the Welsh cause. Instead, the "bitter and twisted" brigade bickered and criticised; and it showed on the field.

As soon as we returned, Ron Waldron was rushed into hospital and a blood clot was found on the lung. The inevitable happened as Ron, against his will, was forced to resign. At the time, it was emphasised that the illness was not "stress related". I have my doubts. A man without faults has not been born, but I doubt if there is anyone as dedicated to the Welsh cause as Ron Waldron.

The Nottingham coach, Alan Davies, was approached

and asked to take over and the management of the Welsh
World Cup team was handed over to my former colleague,
Robert Norster. Both contacted me after I had announced
my resignation, as did several members of the WRU. It was
too late, I was having a private hell of my own.

"There must be more to it than what was printed in the
paper", said one Neath supporter. There was.

Before the Welsh party left for Australia, there had been
questions asked about the wisdom of such a tour. Welsh
rugby had hardly recovered from the disastrous 1988 tour
in New Zealand. I put on a brave face and answered such
questions by arguing that if we didn't compete with the
world's best, then we would have no yardstick. Yet deep
down I knew we were on a hiding to nothing. Wales had
hardly set the world on fire in the Five Nations Championship and I doubted whether we had enough players of
quality to confront the Wallabies.

Lounging in Business Class seats (a most welcome
gesture by the Welsh Rugby Union) we headed for
Australia, knowing that we would be thoroughly examined.
If we didn't know it before, a few video sessions of
Australian provincial rugby should have convinced us.

Ron's methods of training are straightforward. There is
little time for frivolity, because the intensity and the limited
time available don't allow for it. It isn't everyone's cup of
tea, I have to admit that; but I suppose I have become
inured to the challenges of the training sessions. The
bawling out of individuals, if he remembers their names, is
legendary. It disturbs a few players, especially those from
outside the Neath camp, but I've been under other coaches
with different methods and have respected them for their
judgement and integrity. If you are not pulling your weight
with Ron, you'll soon get it in the neck, and from the
beginning of the tour he made his intentions plain. David
Evans of Cardiff was the first to feel the Waldron tongue.
By the end of the tour most of us, including the Neath
players, had been singled out. Some didn't like it, or
couldn't cope with it, and the resentment began.

Rugby is a rough, tough and simple game. That is the

basis of Ron's training methods. My view of the matter is that some of the Welsh players were not dedicated enough to reach their potential in training sessions, let alone the Ballymore Parks of this world. Of the thirty players who went to Australia only twelve were involved in any kind of weight training, and six of those were backs! Little wonder we couldn't take them up front.

Possibly the most discouraging aspect for me was the attitude of the younger players, who seemed to me to act as though the trip was one long holiday. Little wonder that Ron tried to stiffen the training stints. Those who shirked, and there were far too many of them, were singled out. We were after all representing Wales and not some Old Boys Extra "B" boozing trip.

Others were singled out, too. We were told to send Lyn Davies, a reporter with the BBC, to Coventry because his commentary on the game against New South Wales had upset Ron's wife who'd been listening at home. I shall never forget the look on Clive Rowlands face when he was told that Robert, his son-in-law, had been left out of the test match against Australia. He could hardly disguise his anger; but I knew he'd come up against the Waldron wall, and there have been few to penetrate that. Ironically, it was Clive who had handed out the first discipline sermon on tour and the subject of his wrath was Robert. "British Lion, my foot," he shouted at Robert. "I've never been on tour with such a bunch of toss-pots." *C'est la vie.*

The other passengers on board the outgoing flight and the subsequent internal flights of Australia couldn't believe we were the Welsh senior team.

"Is this the Under 21 team or the Under 25s?", we were often asked. Personally, I didn't mind that, but we were a young squad, and there were few old heads to guide the newcomers.

The tour began well enough and the corporate spirit was in good shape. A victory over Western Australia was just the right tonic. Even the damp beds of the Perth hotel didn't diminish our enthusiasm.

"Don't you dare tell the press boys about the damp

beds," shouted Ron, "because your mothers worry more about where you are sleeping rather than with whom."

Yet we knew that the first serious challenge would be against Queensland, and so it proved. All my worst fears about our lack of size and athletic mobility were proved right. Despite a good rally in the second half we were beaten 24–21 because, quite simply, we were not good enough. It was no use pointing the finger at Ron; some of the Welsh players had no regard for pride or motivation, and from then on considered the tour a paid holiday on the lush. Needless to say, it was these individuals who were the first to complain, bicker and find fault elsewhere.

The only solace for some of the players was to be found in late-night pizzas, hardly in line with the dietary schedules given to us before each international season. This again was a source of irritation to me. Our players complain of not being given guidance as to fitness, diets and training plans. I have a small library of them now, but I doubt whether a number of others have even read their copies. You cannot blame the WRU for their lack of information on what a player should expect to have to do before attaining international playing status. Pizzas and a lap or two did not make Simon Poidevin or Willie Ofahengaue the players they are.

My kicking against Western Australia had let me down and three touchline conversions had gone astray. The moments of doubt began, but, true to Sods law, whenever I practised in monsoons or storms, the kicks were going over from everywhere. How can one explain it? I don't know, but Australian supporters are no different from the ones at home. Out came the inevitable question.

"What happened to your kicking today, then?" I just love those observations! I wasn't particularly pleased to hear John Mason of the *Daily Telegraph* during a television commentary observe that I was deliberately slowing down the pace of the game to suit myself. Naturally I assume that John was greased lightning during his playing days.

There were moments of hilarity despite the impending gloom in the camp over what might happen during the rest of the tour. Ron had not appreciated the sight of our locks, Gareth Llewellyn and Paul Arnold, sucking lollipops one day and told them so. It wasn't the picture of the hardened men that Ron wanted us to portray. Inevitably, the squad reacted by purchasing a lollipop each just for Ron's benefit.

The training session after the Queensland defeat became a drain on emotions. After the unity of the early days, the disintegration began. The lectures from Ron had more than a hint of desperation about them.

It didn't help matters that Richard Webster got involved in a fight after a narrow victory against Australia Capital Territories, and a number of the team went "on the town" after the game. It upset Ron greatly that some of the squad were not giving his objectives their full and undivided attention.

The "pommy bastard", Jonathan Davies, turned up at Sydney where we were due to play New South Wales and it was good to see him. He, of course, was playing Rugby League in Australia, but in long conversations with him it became increasingly apparent that he would love to play the Union game again and end his days in a Trimsaran or Llanelli jersey. However, he had made his choice and I doubt very much whether he will ever fulfil his ambition. Yet in Australia, he provided a much-needed tonic for me. The impish humour and leg-pulling at least provided a distraction.

The game against New South Wales proved the old adage that a "big good 'un will always beat a small good 'un". They were an awesome nightmarish sight, brushing us aside from the first moment. Welsh rugby was firmly placed in the cellar basement. We couldn't cope, and we were taken apart. I didn't know what to say, because I knew that our forwards were not in the same league as the likes of the New South Wales pack. It was so devastating, that my thoughts of retiring had begun before the final whistle. Where was our fight, our pride and self-respect? The lessons of that game should have been taught long before we had embarked on such a tour. If the '88 tour of New Zealand had taught us nothing about size, fitness and mobility, here was another classic reminder. The score was New South Wales 70 Wales 6. Ann couldn't believe the scoreline when I phoned. Neither could I. It was a terrifying experience – the more so knowing that there wasn't much we could have done about it once that Australian momentum had gathered speed.

At the after-match function, a local comedian went to town on us. My pasted-on grin became tighter as the evening wore on and the jibes lanced open wounds. Clive Rowlands was furious, and he ranted and raged on the homeward-bound bus. It was all he could do. And we still had Australia to come.

Not even the news that England on tour in Fiji had lost a game was much encouragement. The Monday training session was the worst day of my life since the arrival of my A level results. I disappeared behind a pair of headphones, unsmiling and not really knowing how to get out of such an all-embracing depression. Here we were on the bottom of the world, a once proud rugby-playing nation without a hope or an idea of achieving any measure of respectability. Jonathan Davies tried his best to ginger us up, but you could see on the players' faces and on mine that we had been delivered a mortal blow. Few had any enthusiasm for the final week of the tour.

It got worse. Not even a hilarious pop video recording by Rob Jones, Ieuan Evans, Scott Gibbs and Paul Arnold could lift the clouds of depression. I phoned Ann to tell her that I had made my decision to retire. The long-distance silences became longer.

My father phoned with one of those "hang in there" messages which in the past had done so much to keep everything in perspective. Not this time. I had gone too far for a lifebelt, and I doubt whether I had the will to reach for salvation. It couldn't get worse, I told myself. But it did. As soon as the test team against Australia was announced, those not selected lost all interest. Unity had long gone, and now some of the players were openly challenging Ron.

When Richard Webster was accused of not pulling his weight in a training session, he told Ron. "How would you

145

feel if you'd been kicked in the teeth?" I had some sympathy with Richard since he, and only a few others, had shown the kind of competitive spirit required. Yet, after saying that, I remember Richard arriving on the international scene in the '87 World Cup, straight from playing club rugby in Australia, and taking the place of players who had trained for months for the honour of wearing the Welsh jersey.

I did disagree with the selection for the test match in four places, but I don't think it would have made any real impact on the eventual score. In fact I thought I was rather fortunate to be included, seeing that my form had suffered. We had to go for bulk and brawn, and I would have played Richard Webster in the back row instead of Richie Collins, the Llewellyn brothers at lock and Paul Knight with Mike Griffiths in the front, if only for their experience.

It was no good. The depression wouldn't go away. Not even the exhilarating experience of sitting in the cockpit of the Brisbane-bound flight could completely take away that fear of what was to come. Captain Keith Milner and his crew were exceptionally kind, but the wonderment of it all was only a temporary reprieve. The only relief came from the increasingly frequent phone calls to Ann and hearing Kelly chattering away in the background.

Once the team had been announced there was a distinct rift in the camp and I blew my top with some of the players at a training session. The "bitter and twisted" brigade or the dirt trackers were not pulling their weight at all, and I let rip. The frustrations of the tour were surfacing, and when I had a heated argument with the Pontypridd centre Steele Lewis, who wanted to lay all the blame at Ron's door, it seemed to be the final straw.

I was told that Ron was having a hard time in the press as well. Ron has weaknesses. He cannot remember names, hence Michael Lynagh was dubbed Dai Lynagh throughout the tour. When asked at an early press conference as to whether the Welsh centres would play left and right or inside and outside, Ron's reply was that he didn't know and it didn't matter. I know this is true, because his belief in will allied to fitness is enough. Others may disagree, but at

146

club level you cannot fault his success. Sophisticated he is not, but few coaches are – and I have yet to meet one nominated because of etiquette.

The bad training sessions had a remarkable effect on me. They reinforced my decision to retire, and I was determined to tell the truth on returning home. I found myself in Clive Rowland's room, and the pent-up emotions took over. I broke down. Tears flooded as I told Clive, who listened sympathetically, that I couldn't understand the attitude of some players not wanting to try. Nor could I comprehend how they could be so disloyal to Ron Waldron. The meeting lasted half an hour and Clive explained that he thought Ron had taken too much on. He could coach the team but not also be manager. The demands of the job were too much for one individual. He argued that I was needed, that respect had to be gained and there were people dependent on my level-headedness on the field.

I left Clive's room feeling no better. In fact, I was embarrassed. The remaining hours before meeting Australia were spent either shopping or watching television. I couldn't sleep, continually phoning home until two o'clock in the morning and watching the Wimbledon finals until the early hours. Great preparation!

The match was a nightmare. I lost the toss. It was about the only part of the afternoon we had an even chance of winning. I dropped a high ball in the early minutes and Australia scored. It was the beginning of the yellow avalanche. The game plan of keeping the ball alive to give our centres an opportunity of penetrating the Australian defences disappeared with the alacrity of a Russian coup. The gulf was enormous. It was men against boys and I should apologise to the lads for my own performance on that day. We simply couldn't cope, and players like Willie Ofahengaue, Simon Poidevin and Tim Gavin gave us a lesson in being aware of positional play. Gradually we lost all heart, myself included, and that Australian hooter could not come soon enough.

Of course, I managed to end my career on a stupid note. In I went to tackle Ofanghaue, and soon discovered why he's called the "Tongan Torpedo". His knee went into my thigh, and that was it.

There were thoughts of the phone calls, the dissent within the camp and the spectacle of some who hadn't tried since arriving in Australia. To compete with the Wallabies, there would have to be a complete overhaul of Welsh thinking. It was 23–6 when I left the field. Sitting in the stand was even more distressing. The Australians did their version of the Mexican wave, a Welsh supporter clad in a Red Dragon flag was pelted with beer cans as the Wallabies piled on the points. The press conference was going to be a difficult one.

I made the right noises about the amount of work that had to be done and the enormous challenge ahead. At the back of my mind, I had no fight left in me. The night before had been almost sleepless in a room which creaked with the rising temperatures. There would be many more to follow if I stayed. Perhaps some of the youngsters could with time erase the memory of what had happened. I had been through it all before in the '87 World Cup against New Zealand. Presentations were made to our kind liaison officers at the hotel and there was just one function to go before that homeward-bound flight.

The official post-match dinner started off pleasantly enough with Nick Farr-Jones, the Australian captain, admitting that he would retire at the end of the '91 World Cup. His speech, as I would expect from a solicitor, was an honest one, underlining how much work we had to do to raise standards so that each player could look the other in the eye. Few apart from Emyr Lewis that afternoon had shown any of the qualities that Nick mentioned – myself included.

On the other tables, the Welsh lads were getting out of order. A mini-rugby ball was thrown over the tables and landed in a soup bowl in front of one of the guests' wives. I just prayed that the dinner would be over quickly. Kevin Phillips, who had been sharing a table with David Campese, though the latter had hardly consumed the same amount of beverage as our hooker, was about to create havoc. I had seen it before and I knew trouble was brewing.

First, Kevin wanted to have words with referee David Bishop and then Fred Howard of England. Kevin had a long-standing argument to settle with Fred after the Neath/All Blacks game at the Gnoll. Fortunately, I was able to usher David away and Fred found a safe haven somewhere else.

Suddenly, a row broke out between Kevin, Gareth Llewellyn, Mike Hall and Emyr Lewis. The subject, I was told, was the writing of Paul Rees in the *South Wales Echo* and the subsequent attacks on Ron as Welsh coach. I don't think it really mattered what was being debated. Something was going to erupt that night because the temperature had been simmering for so long. Clive Rowlands and I attempted to step in, but there is little reason in drink and I joined Campese on the balcony.

The skirmish which broke out was apparently short and sharp, the end result being a broken glass and Mike Hall's cut hand. Malcolm Downes, the team doctor, attended to the injury, but the harm to Welsh rugby was incalculable. Here we were, the clowns of international rugby both on and off the field. We were a disgrace in every sense and I was ashamed to be a Welshman. How in God's name were we to have any respect? Not even the complimentary words from David Bishop and former Wallaby, Greg Martin, who argued that I should stay in international rugby, were enough to wipe the memory of such a disaster from my mind, let alone the front pages of the newspapers. If the publicity was bad, then we deserved it and no ranting or raving from Clive Rowlands on the bus could alter the immense damage caused. We were boys in a man's land, but we had acted like tots.

Discipline had been wrecked, despite the "managerial" presence of Ron, Clive, two selectors and two Presidents of the Welsh Rugby Union. You would have thought that the night had been traumatic enough, but the boys headed for a nightclub in Brisbane. I gave back the beer kitty to Clive, some three hundred Australian dollars, because I wanted no part of what appeared to be a dangerous night. Instead, I went back to the hotel, ordered a plate of sandwiches and waited for the welcome voices of Ann and my brother, Andy, on the phone.

The phone rang. Andy argued that I shouldn't announce my retirement until I had given it enough time and thought after returning home.

"Woeful Wales Wallop Each Other" said the morning headline. I couldn't wait for that plane and a bit of peace. My mind was made up.

11

My Way

Whether by design or not, the Rugby World Cup of 1987 revolutionised many aspects of the game. It was the brainchild of the Southern Hemisphere, the progressive lot who knew something needed to be done to keep rugby at the forefront of sports marketing and appeal. New Zealand rugby had been having a bad press because of injuries to youngsters, and in the land of the White Cloud where babies are said to be born with silver ferns instead of spoons, the authorities were worried about the decline in popularity. Something had to be done. A new game was adopted from Argentina, and adapted for youngsters. It was a non-tackling game, devoid of risks and full of running. It caught on, and the "New Image" rugby of New Zealand eventually became "Waller Rugby" in Australia, "Leprechaun Rugby" in Ireland, "Tulip Rugby" in Holland and "Dragon Rugby" in Wales.

Senior rugby needed a new marketing edge, too. The appeal of the game in New Zealand had been built on the admirable All Black supremacy on the world rugby stage. So they needed a revitalised platform. Not only did they command that stage, they also visualised a theatre to house it. It was called the World Cup.

You didn't have to tell the Aussies about marketing, since they had seen the transformation of cricket under Kerry Packer. They were willing partners, because rugby was still only the fifth most popular sport in Australia and anything which would capture world headlines was welcome. Besides, it was time to show the Five Nations closeted brigade that they were capable of leading the game both on and off the field.

So the World Cup was born, with television exposure in place, sponsors willing to foot bills and vast sums of untapped revenue to be exploited; but the players realised, what they had feared before, that the one ingredient missing in this new and imaginative initiative was concern for them. The Unions would reap massive financial dividends if the concept worked and the players who attracted the punters in the first place would be well down in the pecking order when it came to considering compensation for weeks and hours lost – not only for turning up for the fête but for the toil in preparing for it. The last to be considered would be their employers. Various strictures were laid down to us in tablets of IRB stone as to what we could and could not do as rugby internationals. Or so we were led to believe. Every bulletin issued by the International Rugby Board seemed to contain contradictory statements. Vested interests were playing a major role in defining the parameters of conduct as far as endorsements and earnings from the game was concerned. No one in Wales had realised what was happening abroad.

We soon came to terms with it, because on arrival in the Southern Hemisphere for the '87 World Cup the first television commercial we saw featured the All Blacks advertising beer. Steve McDowell and John Kirwan were to be seen all over New Zealand on advertisement hoardings, and we wanted to know how could they get away with it. Apart from the challenge of the event itself, it was one of the major talking points in the British camps. When we got home, we said, something would be done.

In my opinion this seemed like open exploitation of the game and we were not so naive as to think that the fees received were being ploughed into the game. Some players had established companies to reap the benefits of the market; others created trusts, a thinly disguised form of hoarding money for the eventual day. It was staggering, to say the least, and a long way down the road towards open professionalism. We had heard of covert deals in France, we knew of healthy mileage expenses in Wales, jobs that didn't exist in Italy; but this was something else. No longer would we suggest, as had been practised since the 70s that cheques for interviews should be deposited in your wife's or father's name. Alas, little has been done, and though we now have agents for squads and individuals, the arguments still rage as to whether players should receive payments for playing. The traditionalists will not have it, on principle, because it would destroy the foundations and pillars of the game. They didn't get a penny, so why should the modern player benefit? Nor are the clubs too anxious to sponsor the paid ranks, though goodness knows there are enough clubs doing it already in various ways. Huge transfer fees exist in South African and French rugby, and smaller inducements in Welsh rugby – and a principal English club was prepared recently to offer £30,000 to a Welsh player to cross the border.

No, the players will not name the individuals concerned nor the amounts floating around club rugby, both at senior and junior level. The underworld of payment has been forced on rugby by the hypocritical and inconsistent application of the laws all over the world. It happens in Wales as well. That is why the half-way house of semi-professionalism would never work. That would invite envy and bad practices.

You would have to be fairly naive not to know which clubs are paymasters and which are not. Cardiff, for instance, have always insisted that they are above all of this: but what is a sponsored car if not payment for services rendered? Why did so many Bath players cross the Severn Bridge to join Newport when the leagues were introduced in Wales with the proud Black and Ambers facing a season in the second division? We are to presume it was the attraction of playing at Rodney Parade and not at the Bath Recreation Ground.

The sports goods salesmen are everywhere offering kit and deals, company days and every other kind of inducement. What are these but payments of a kind? Neath, my own club, award the squad players mileage allowances and an allowance for match and training days. The amount wouldn't make a bank manager nor a bookie blink.

153

The real concentration of rugby finance is controlled by the International Rugby Board and its creation the Rugby World Cup Ltd. Though it is now a global game, only the elite are allowed entry into this private club. They keep their financial cards so close to their chests that they are always in danger of being accused of ignoring the poor and fattening the wallets of the richer nations.

It is a club whose ramparts, so far, the rest of the rugby-playing world has yet to breach – apart from superficial handouts and recognition from time to time. The game is supposedly played in some 150 countries but I doubt whether the International Board was responsible for spreading the gospel. It was more likely a rugby fanatic – priest, teacher, railway worker or farmer – who had little interest in or knowledge of world rugby politics. These people are a world away from the decision-makers.

When the UK and France World Cup was launched, we heard of impressive projected surplus profits of fifty million pounds plus. The surplus, we were told, would go towards the development of the game. It sounded fine, until stories emerged in the press that some countries could not afford to compete in their qualifying groups, whereas the moguls of international rugby and their chosen marketing companies were touring the country in luxury hotels and dining on the projected proceeds on a nightly basis. Suddenly, the projected figures became less impressive, with the war in the Gulf to blame and also a major recession. Was it so necessary to engage so many seemingly high-profile companies to organise and market the event and to be accountable to so few?

You couldn't blame the companies concerned for attracting the interest of the Rugby World Cup authorities and blinding them with attractive promises. Yet, did these same companies have any experience of Rugby Union football's immense complexities and the way it straddles amateurism and commerce? Even one of the A 470 wandering sheep could have predicted that expensive hospitality offers would not appeal at Pontypridd and Pontypool. The merchandisers complained because the pirate T-shirt and emblem makers were coining it. Was it ever going to be otherwise? And who will pursue the litigation? There are so many questions to be asked; and as supporters, players and unpaid custodians of the game, we have to pose the most painful and most unanswerable question of all. Is the game in safe hands, and can we leave it in the hands of the incumbents, who might just as well say, "You don't expect me to know about that, after all I'm only a rugby player at heart"?

To hide behind such false naivety does the game no good at all. Even in dealing with the world's media, there was contempt for the intruder. The handling of the Daniel Dubroca incident, when he attacked the New Zealand referee David Bishop during the last World Cup, was pathetic. For a national coach to have behaved in such a way was disgraceful and justice should have been swift. However, the chairman of the Rugby World Cup Russ Thomas in stating that the matter was closed at a press conference in Lille, did the game and its reputation, I think, immense harm. Subsequently the matter was re-opened, Dubroca resigned, but to the onlooker it suggested that the game was being run by people who could not, or did not want to face reality. For Dubroca to claim that his actions and the dismissal of the French were directly attributable to the British press was so far removed from reality that it was laughable. There was obviously an incident in the tunnel, but for the authorities to attempt to ignore the matter was, in my view, shameful.

How many of the game's supporters who pay at the turnstiles for the World Cup will ever see a true balance sheet of the World Cup expenditure? Yet these people are the lifeblood of our game, and not the self-perpetuating rugby moguls holding court on anything from the differential penalty to the next Duck à l'Orange. They should be accountable to all of us, and not the chosen few.

The shop window of the game is undoubtedly the World Cup and International rugby. Like Christians fed to the commercial lions, the players are totally unaware of the finances generated by these events, and the East India Club brigade would argue until cherub-faced that we have no business to know either. To keep the people who support the game at arm's length is to invite animosity.

The necessity of having qualified, professional people to run the game is obvious. We are in a television age which is constantly changing but still has an insatiable appetite for sport, and where huge fees are discussed for exclusive rights, sponsorship deals and the marketing of merchandise. The gradual and sometimes painful introduction of marketing and commercial executives has been a welcome development, but they are accountable to well-meaning but sometimes self-interested amateurs. It is inconceivable for a multi-million-pound business to be administered on a voluntary basis. I'm sure the Blue Chip companies of the Stock Exchange are not run on these lines, and if the organisation of rugby football is to survive, it has to be equipped with professionally qualified people appointed from within the game. I would stress that every one of these executives should have an interest in the game, not as a market to be exploited but as a pursuit followed by so many who are unable to afford the ever increasing prices for Twickenham and Cardiff.

Imagine what Tony O'Reilly would do for the game if he ever, in retirement, could be persuaded to take on the task. At Neath, the club after much discussion, has appointed Brian Thomas as Manager. But the structure by no means allows him a free hand to develop. If he were found wanting, he could be sacked; but frequent committee meetings are a hindrance to anyone who wants to get to grips with age-old problems. Rugby, knowing that it has had to react at international and club level, has taken the easy course, by looking at London-based companies. What on earth does a marketing or television company immersed in professional sports like soccer, golf or tennis know about the structure of rugby?

Far too many marketing companies who wouldn't know a ruck from a maul have been lured into the game, especially at the top level, but the result is that the game has become too expensive for the man who has devoted a lifetime to looking after the Extra "B" team on chilly Saturday afternoons. The quest to attract the so-called A.B.

reader of the south-east will eventually, if it has not happened already, deny the die-hard follower his access to the international arenas. He and his like are an endangered species, because the inevitable will happen and he'll become disenchanted with the marketing hype of those who see rugby union football as a mere vehicle for company expansion or a prestige addition to their client lists.

Only time will tell if the money generated by the World Cup will find its way into improved facilities at grounds and better development at school and youth level on a global basis. One can only hope that it does. If it doesn't, those responsible for its organisation will pay a greater debt than all the money generated by hospitality packages, television fees and merchandising – that of guilt. I fear, though, we will never know.

Should players be paid for playing the game? With the liberalisation of the laws governing amateurism, in Wales a player is allowed to market himself individually and as part of his national squad. The interpretation of this change varies considerably, not only between Hemispheres but within the Five Nations. It is an absolute mess. If the player is good enough and has worked hard enough to achieve international status then he will attract fees for appearances and product advertising. That is his reward for all those lonely years of weight training, wet coaching sessions, road running and time devoted to the sport. To play for one's country should not be contaminated by financial induce-ments. Ask a young boy in Wales playing "Dragon Rugby": he would give his right arm to run on to the Arms Park pitch with fifty thousand cheering him on. There is no greater reward than that.

However, if the administrators continue to be so secretive and so divorced from the players, the frustration will continue. That became abundantly apparent when the England players botched their plans to become a marketing entity. They realised what an attractive proposition they might be to a potential client, but jealousy and mis-understanding saw the whole matter disintegrate into a public shambles. The RFU could not understand what might possibly be the matter with Messrs Moore and

157

Carling, despite repeated assurances that lines of communication were open.

In truth they haven't been open since William Webb Ellis questioned authority and broke the rules. The England team, however embarrassingly misguided, did exactly that in questioning authority, and I have doubts whether Twickenham will ever be the same.

What of France, where tales of professionalism are so commonplace that the man who plays the game for the love of it is considered stupid? When a leading professional rugby league club, Le Pontet, changes codes to Union without a murmur of protest from the International Board, credibility goes out through the window. Payment, expenses, fees, call it what you will, has always been rumoured to be the norm in France, and their only response is the raising of arms and protests of innocence. Did the French players really insist on thousands of pounds as bonus money in the last World Cup, or was this newspaper talk? I suspect that this time, the journalists were right – but did we hear any comment from the RWC on what was rumoured to be a breach of the laws? Their response would undoubtedly be that they have no brief to examine or investigate rumours: this leaves everyone suspecting that the authorities don't want to deal with such unsavoury practices.

In Wales, once the land of cloth-capped knuckle fighting, badger-baiting and house-buying for successful rugby players, matters are just as complex. Contrary to rumours, most clubs haven't got the capital to reimburse their players. If they had, I don't think half the players we lost in the late 80s would have been tempted North. The money simply isn't there, and if there are financial inducements it doesn't take an Inspector Morse to guess where the Welsh financial pots are located. We lack capital; but our lack of leadership is far more crucial to the game's future.

As captain of my country, I wasn't aware of half of what was going on at the WRU. It didn't matter really, because as a player the last thing you want to do is to get embroiled in the politics of committees. I didn't know half of them: but that was my fault, since that Waldron disease of forgetting names has also affected me. The constant changes at the WRU have not helped sustain continuity or provide the opportunity of getting to know them. The traditionalists will linger on at committee level until the Almighty calls them, and the younger members are too concerned with survival to think of visionary progress. The paid administrators are always subject to the accountable whims of the Committee and sub-committees. The structure of the WRU has been founded on survival and jealousy, the clannish politics of the clubs, with success stumbled upon rather than developed. Hopefully, with the introduction of Technical Officers and an army of Development officers, the game will stand a reasonable chance of progress.

The mood has to be expansive and visionary, since there have been so many forgettable years, barren of thought. Is the WRU Committee capable of such vision? For some Committee members, not all, it seemed to me as though the ultimate reward might be to get on a Paris or Edinburgh all-expenses trip. For the chosen few they might even travel further afield. In 1991 Wales took two Presidents to Australia.

I have never quite understood the need for a new President every year. It is undoubtedly an honour, but the office of the Presidency could be far more effective if it had some continuity. Better to have a figurehead, an ambassador if you like, than an individual nominated on an annual basis, because that is the way the system works. Since 1953 the Presidency of the WRU has been based on nomination from within the Union. It is unworkable, and I would suggest that the constitution should be changed and that the office of the Presidency should carry the weight of a chairman of the Board of Governors, answerable to the Union, and nominated by the Union, but not necessarily from within the Union.

Hopefully, the structure of the Union will change dramatically over the next couple of years. Paid professionals are needed to lead commercial, technical, media and development departments, with the Chief Executive as the Managing Director.

This structure or Board could then be answerable to a Committee nominated by the member clubs. It is a structure that we need; but my only fear is that those appointed would come from within the Union, the very people whose inactivity over the last two decades has prompted the necessity of a structural revolution. We need professionals, and not political or Masonic appointees.

Yet, the real culprit in Wales is the player. I have argued for players to be involved in the decision-making process and was delighted to be invited on to the WRU Committee concerned with the relaxation of the amateur laws. I didn't learn a great deal; but, fresh from the international playing fields, I would hope to have more involvement, in order to rectify the total imbalance of players' representation.

I am uneasy about one aspect. To represent the players should be the pinnacle for me, so why the hesitation? If my demands were for better communication, more under-standing of the player's needs, innovative yet demanding training schedules, a plentiful supply of kit, consideration for the players' wives and girlfriends. . . . I would champion these demands with intense fervour and would to the point of revolt make sure they were met.

There lies the problem. They have been. The kit has been plentiful, the wives and girlfriends now travel on away trips during the Five Nations Championship, players are now given tests and targets for achieving fitness levels.

Much to my disgust, the response from the players has been to say the least disappointing, and in some cases quite unworthy. I think it was Mike Watkins, as Welsh captain, when asked after an Arms Park defeat where the result left Welsh rugby, retorted, "Back at the Angel Hotel for a good few pints". I assume he said it in jest, but unfortunately it is a remark whose truth has been too often confirmed.

The defects in my own game are apparent to me. I do not need anyone to tell me, and if I have played a bad game, there is no one in that ground or stadium who knows it better. The criticism of the lack of speed in my game prompted a course of action. Dave Crottie, an Australian fitness expert, was asked to give a fitness schedule, far more demanding than any of the plans handed down by the

Union. This involved countless hours on my own, sometimes supervised by Ann's stopwatch, and the result was
astonishing. I could last the pace of a game much better,
last a series of games with something in reserve, and found
my speed had improved dramatically. To my regret I
invited Dave down to Wales to see if Welsh business and
industry would sponsor a few more of the Welsh players on
such a rigid fitness and peak schedule. Despite television
and newspaper coverage, not a single Welsh company came
forward. Yet on match days, the hospitality marquees are
full of opinionated worthies bemoaning the lack of basic
fitness and strength in the Welsh side.

The Union, during my playing career, sent out three
fitness schedules, individually tailored for each member of
the squad. I doubt whether some of the players ever opened
their envelopes. Why some of the Welsh players seem to
believe they are above all of this defeats me. Very few of my
contemporaries truly comprehend what is demanded of
them physically if we are to compete at the highest levels. It
is no good beginning your training in August with a few
runs and then puffing around for the first two months of the
season; and it is no good depending on club coaching
sessions to supplement the lack of personal schedules. It
has to be worked upon, and the aspiring international who
hasn't spent the countless lonely hours in working on his
maximum achievement levels doesn't deserve a cap. Unfortunately, Wales has capped too many unfit players who
haven't the remotest idea of what I'm talking about. There
are some at Neath who have convinced themselves that
sheer size alone is enough to merit national attention. They
are only fools to themselves, in my opinion, and they look
foolish when thrust against the challenges of Australians
and New Zealanders.

I look with admiration at the likes of Gary Whetton,
Wayne Shelford, Simon Poidevin, who have allied physique
and fitness over a vast number of years. They know what it
takes, and have been doing it for the best part of a decade.
That takes tremendous dedication and will, and the reward
is being able to compete with the best without fear of fitness
limitations.

Unfortunately, it is the vogue in Wales to attack the coach if he is unsuccessful. There are no escape routes, only the exit sign. Without fear of contradiction, I know that Tony Gray, John Ryan and Ron Waldron would have had far more successful careers had the Welsh players stopped moaning about coaching directives and arrived at sessions in peak physical shape. Few did, and the coaches were sacked. It should have been the other way. And that is why I feel a little hesitant about players' representation. They have to give in order to receive.

To hear some of our players moan about the training methods adopted in Australia made me angry. The squad was primarily based on Neath players, who knew what to expect from Ron Waldron. The Cardiff boys didn't like it, since their idea of training seems to be built on a sense of fun. The sessions were hard because the players were not fit enough. In order to compensate for this Ron employed rigid and demanding exercises which didn't go down well with the boys; they wanted a game of touch rugby to get things moving. How we expect to live with the Wallabies and All Blacks on a basis of a few jogs and a game of touch rugby I'll never know. It is the responsibility of the player to be fit enough at the beginning of the session. Unfortunately few of the Welsh players realise this, and the forwards are particularly guilty. For some reason the forwards have convinced themselves that only the three-quarters need concentrate on speed and fitness. The attitude of some of them defies description.

On the field of play itself, we have witnessed a vast number of changes in the laws of the game. The admirable intent of making rugby a far more open and running expression of skills has not always worked and the law makers have to be very careful before they tinker and touch, especially those laws which are so open to differences of interpretation. If there is one thing that frustrates the modern player it is the huge variance in interpretation expressed, not between the Northern and the Southern Hemisphere, but between referees who might be officiating at Neath one Saturday and Aberavon the next. There is nothing more annoying than having to play to one man's reading and view of the game rather than to a consistent adaptation of law.

There have been improvements: gradually, the advantage law seems to have come to be fairly applied. But in other areas it is difficult to recognise the game from one Saturday to the next. I have never been able to find a referee who can fully explain his decisions on the collapsing of the scrum. One will tell you that he's watching the binding, the other examines the feet positions and some tell you that they instinctively recognise the guilty party.

The penalty for foul play is another area where some referees are strict and will not tolerate any skullduggery and there are others, fearful of an assessor in the stand, who will either turn a blind eye to the short punch and straying foot, or resort to a final warning or glance. It is no good: if there is a plea – and I'm sure the referees are just as keen to adopt a common code – then guidelines have to be observed and consistency adopted. There is no place for foul play in rugby union, and those responsible – some on a regular basis – should be punished accordingly. The game, in the modern context, is hard enough without this kind of thing, and the stud merchant can't be of any help to his team if he's indulging in some personal psychopathic vendetta. Unfortunately, there are too many of them around.

Much has been written and discussed about the re-evaluation of the try. Some support the increasing of its value or decreasing the value of the penalty. This is a particularly popular argument in Scotland, and would receive support in Wales since there seems to be a misguided notion that it is desirable to be at the forefront of what is called progressive thinking if nothing can be achieved on the field. The intention, once again, is to introduce a greater prize for a more expansive game. No matter how admirable such intentions are, I believe that to alter the points system would have a detrimental effect on the game.

There is little doubt that, canny as the modern player is, he would become more cynical in the knowledge that the opposition by scoring a try could gain five and maybe seven points with the conversion. I have little doubt that it would lead to far more infringements, especially at attacking scrums and line-outs. Far better to give away a three-point penalty in desperation than surrender to a seven-point try. It might also lead to other cynical fouls. We have seen enough of what might happen already at all levels of rugby. I have stressed elsewhere that I have no truck with those who attempt to maim and hurt by foul deeds. The kick aimed at someone's head or any part of the body, the punch thrown and, worst of all, the gouging of eyes does not belong in this sport. If the offence is worthy of a sending-off then so be it, but if the incident is serious enough to warrant a warning penalty then the kick should be taken before the offending team's posts. I have never been able to fathom why a penalty for an offence, committed in one area of the field, should secure three points and the very same offence, at times more severe, in another part, a mere kick to touch. This change would, I believe, eradicate the cynicism, and go a long way to helping cowardly clubs to dispense with the thugs who roam around looking for their Saturday afternoon victims.

There will be those who will say that Wales and Neath have selected such individuals. I would agree with them. Selectors at all levels have a duty not to pick persistent offenders. Those entrusted with the game's discipline and punishments also have their responsibilities. Here again we have inconsistencies of immense proportions. How can we in Wales complain when a player banned *sine die* by the Union was appointed assistant coach at a leading club? Kevin Moseley was banned for stamping on the French threequarter, Andrieu, for thirty-two weeks, considerably more than anyone else in International rugby sent off for a similar offence. When Wales toured Namibia, the local officials argued that Andre Stoop, the local full-back, should be reinstated immediately after being sent off for punching. It once again prompts the questions: where is the uniformity and where is the guidance?

You wouldn't expect me, of all people, to devalue the penalty, but I would agree with any constructive changes in order to speed up the game. The law makers must be made aware of, or at least try to think through, the consequences of their actions. For instance, the law which allows a player to be within ten metres of his opponent when catching the ball is absurd. I would prefer to revert to the old law, whereby the kicker or any player behind him is the only individual allowed to play his team "on side". The introduction of the ten-metre law has confused so many players and referees, and the result is inevitably a kick to touch by your opponent, a subsequent line-out and another stoppage. At least, when the old law was in operation, it allowed the opposing team to counter-attack, since at least the kicker and his supportive runners would be out of position.

Nor am I in favour of the current thinking that the evolution of the game will eventually dispense with line-outs. Shambolic and arbitrary as they have been, owing more than anything to referees opting out and players taking full advantage of such liberal behaviour, they are a vital part of the game – vital in the sense that I have always believed rugby to be a game for all sizes and skills.

There is immense skill in the well-timed, two-handed catch and the physics of a driven scrum is sheer geometric pressure when properly applied. It is only the abuse of the laws which have degraded the skills: the barging at the line-out, the sneaky skills of jersey-pulling, foot-stamping and waving elbows, that so many are adept at using. Firm refereeing with a little help from the laws would once again see the line-out as an attacking restart to the game rather than the unproductive mayhem it has become. I would be interested to see the effect of the line-out being reduced to six or possibly five men with the same amount of space being given to its formation and stricter application of the distances between players being introduced. I remember Clive Norling at the outset of a season declaring his intention of refereeing only the correct distances as stated by the laws when confronted by a line-out. He stuck to it because it worked. With the absence of a general scramble, the practice of leaning on players disappeared, and the result was a game relatively free of penalties. He can get away with it since his instructions are crystal-clear and like his England contemporary Fred Howard, he will not suffer fools. Unfortunately, other referees are intimidated by major games and partisan crowds, and the concentration simply goes.

At the moment at all levels, the game has become a platform for spoilers – the lifters and blockers, who are at best playing to the referee's interpretation, and, at worst, denying their own skills.

We have South Africa arguing the case for legalising lifting and there is some merit in attempting to clean up what has been called the illegitimate child of the game. This however reduces the role of the supporting prop to a virtual "lifting" extra. I don't believe this to be the answer; but certainly there is an urgent need to dictate what is allowed and what isn't. When Wales toured in Namibia our forwards practised their lifting techniques for the provincial games whereas Namibia, because of Fred Howard's presence, adopted "legal" techniques for the test matches. It was a ridiculous situation. There is an urgent demand for consistency so that players know where they stand.

The different interpretations leave the player no alternative but to play to the referee and not the law. New Zealand and Scotland when breaking from a scrum invariably protect the ball carrier by impeding the path of the tackler. It is accepted in American Football but should not be allowed in rugby. Until action replays were watched by the referees, only then did it become apparent how much obstruction there is in threequarter movements, especially if the attacking side has called a mis-move or a dummy. It happens so quickly, and I for one sympathise with the referee: he will be criticised if he makes the game static and castigated if he doesn't penalise.

The commendable introduction of neutral touch judges at major games, including leagues, needs to be extended; but even here there has been a huge disparity in levels of observation. I have witnessed fouls which have been committed in front of touchline officials, yet the flag has stayed down: and then another official might flag for a trivial offence on the other side of the field. Again, there has to be uniformity and the sooner all rugby is officiated by neutral officials the better. We still have our own touch judge at Neath who is infamous for his generosity in awarding dubious kicks and elasticated yardage on the touchlines. Although it has caused amusement over the years to the home supporters and resentment for our visitors, the games, certainly at Cup and League level, have become too competitive to be decided by the whim of a "home bird," no matter how much mirth he generates.

We are at the threshold of the twenty-first century and it would be comforting to know that the game is prepared for the challenges of the next hundred years. I myself have serious doubts, because there are so many inconsistencies and anomalies in administration, development and facilities.

Whereas, in Wales, clubs like Cardiff, Neath and Llanelli have ambitious plans, few clubs elsewhere can afford to be as expansive. It isn't simply a matter of attracting hospitality clients for them; the seasonal battle to meet travelling costs is enough of a headache. Somehow, the clubs will have to receive assistance from the parent body; otherwise the inevitable will happen, and the growth of a super league on a European or Anglo-Welsh basis will emerge.

The player has his needs: adequate training facilities and medical supervision, the time to develop and work on his personal fitness. The ill-lit weights room with second-hand bars and bells bought from receivership stock will have to become a thing of the past. Junior clubs, too, will be forced to respond to their responsibilities if they are to retain the services of promising players. It isn't all about inflated expenses. The player of today is only too well aware of what other sports have to offer, and the days of the Welsh village with church, chapels, two pubs and the rugby club are over. That village now probably enjoys a close proximity to a leisure centre, with a wide spectrum of sports to attract the keen enthusiast.

Change is inevitable, but the speed of reaction is vital. Had the Safety of Sports Grounds Act not forced our major clubs to redesign and carry out renovations, it is arguable whether many of the Welsh grounds would have altered their appearance since the days when pig bladders were kicked around. The spectator needs to be comforted and courted. If you have seen the sports clubs of Europe, the excellent facilities of Australian sports centres, it is enough to make you weep. We are light years away from the progressive countries who have ensured that generations of families will want more and more leisure facilities.

The Gnoll, despite the odd coat of paint, hasn't changed at all and is ill-equipped to meet the sporting demands of local youngsters. The Arms Park, pride of the Welsh Rugby Union, is still a hamburger-and-hot-dog stadium on International days, unless you know someone who knows someone who can get you into a cold buffet reception. These are the premier grounds of Wales. Cater for the pie-and-chips supporter by all means: but is it not desirable to make our grounds centres of sporting excellence for the whole community?

Where are the running tracks, the swimming pools, restaurants, crèches, adventure playgrounds, practice fields, gymnasiums, tennis, squash and badminton courts? This is rugby's problem. We have to extend the appeal for the younger generation. It used to fill this vacuum when there was little else on offer, but the years in the sand have left an awful lot of work to be done in order to catch up with our responsibilities, let alone keep ahead of the competition.

"I'll tell you what we'll do, Paul. We'll extend the bar. That should bring in some extra cash, especially on Bingo night!"

12

World Cup '91

It was quite breathtaking, the whole event. It was difficult to take it all in, but one thing became clear: rugby football, thanks to the media – and, in particular, television – was no longer the poor relation of the sports world. Throughout the land and across the world images of great players, moves, moments and emotions were sent into the homes of people who might otherwise never have seen a rugby game in their lives. I was thrilled by every moment, apart from witnessing the Welsh demise.

On the afternoon of the England–New Zealand match it was reported that the financial city of London came to a halt; there was a ticker-tape reception for the Australians as they returned home; and a capacity crowd turned up at a Western Samoan football ground to watch satellite pictures of their team upsetting Wales and Argentina.

For my part, I couldn't get enough. The domestic chores were ignored, there was a half-painted room during the Ireland and Australian match, and suddenly it was all over. The rain descended on cue a few minutes after the final whistle at Twickenham, leaving the smoked salmon sandwiches of the West Car Park a little damp – but few cared. It was one glorious competitive event from start to finish.

Of course, there were heroes; and who would deny David Campese his right to the "man of the tournament" title? If, as I said before, my appreciation of him was confined to television viewing, here he was now, combining wit, athleticism and speed to devastating effect. There are few men who draw that breath of expectancy when they receive the ball. When Campese took delivery it was more of a gasp than a held breath. Such was his impact. He was going to retire, like so many of the other players. Now he's changed his mind and I'm delighted that another generation will be granted the opportunity of watching him in action.

Why was it that, even under pressure as they were in the mud of Pontypool or in front of the partisan Irish at Lansdowne Road you always felt the Australians had a move or a surge in hand? Perhaps they haven't achieved their potential and maybe the injuries to Nick Farr-Jones did inhibit their style. I just want to be around when all the factors come into force. There won't be a team to match them, no matter what the bars of Cape Town and Durban may say.

Did I regret not being a part of this greatest of rugby feasts? Yes, I did, but I didn't miss being involved in the Welsh camp. The only tinge of regret I had was watching that majestic clash between Ireland and Australia at Lansdowne Road. I would have loved to be part of that Irish team and of the international stage. They knew that they were beaten for running skills, and on paper they were short of ball-winning forwards in the line-outs and scrums. In fact they should not have been in contention at all. They had lost just about every preparatory game including two tests against Namibia and a woeful display at Gloucester. Here they were, though, with minutes to go – and then came that marvellous, inspiring run by Gordon Hamilton in front of the leading side of the summer. They played like men possessed, and Steve Smith, the hooker, had his finest game ever.

I was astonished to hear our own ex-international J. J. Williams on the radio describe the Irish team as having no class players but bags of commitment. It was an affront to the Irish from a man who enjoyed success which was dependent on pace rather than skill. For the Irish to have such commitment, to have been so unyielding, left me, and I'm sure the rest of the rugby world, warming to them as the game progressed. It just showed what could be accomplished by a team which believed that the impossible could be achieved. It made me angry, too, for I knew that the

Welsh had folded so badly to the Australians, not only during the summer but also at Cardiff in the World Cup.

For me it was the game of the tournament, with passion, drama and quality play from the Australians, who had surely had the fright of their lives on seeing this swarm of green jerseys challenge their supremacy. On paper, I don't think there is a huge gap between the ability of Wales and Ireland. Yet there is a world of difference between the one team which is satisfied with mediocrity and the other who will have none of it. I tried to carry on with the decorating during the game, but early in the first half the paint had dried on the brush.

There were classic moments to savour and individuals to admire. There is little doubt that apart from the electric running skills of Australia and the efficiency of New Zealand, England and Scotland did the Northern Hemisphere proud.

To have reached the final of the Rugby World Cup was a measure of England's single-minded approach to achieving their potential. I don't think they were a great team, far from it, but at least they did achieve what they were capable of achieving, especially against Scotland in the semi-final. It wasn't pretty to watch, but no one would deny its effectiveness. If they were lambasted by the press for being too stereotyped and boring, they at least reached the final; whereas the flamboyant French failed and the inspired Scots didn't manage the last lap. The pack gave England a splendid platform for Richard Hill and Rob Andrew, and though I had some misgivings about the quality of their centre play, who could deny England their efficiency?

I have a sneaking suspicion, though, that the "boring" labels did get to them, because there was more than a suggestion in the final that they were caught between two strategies. They ran when they should have kicked and kicked when the ball screamed to be sent wide. This surely was a matter of Rob Andrew and his captain being at odds with the tactical game plan. Rob received the ball forty-one times and distributed twenty-six times. Michael Lynagh in opposition only passed on four occasions out of the seventeen times he received the ball. If the Australians, and in particular Lynagh, taught us one thing, that was the value

171

of the tactical kick, either to gain ground or to place the opposition under pressure. I wonder why England adopted such tactics; the basics had served them well until then.

If there was one player in the England camp who caught my eye it was full-back Jonathan Webb. He was outstanding, especially in the opening game against New Zealand. The positioning was good, but the temperament was even better. He'd have been forgiven for a little hesitancy, since his selection had caused a few eyebrows to be raised after the success of Simon Hodgkinson with the boot during the previous season. He justified his elevation and hardly put a foot wrong.

Much has been written about the ageing England team. It is true that, for example, Probyn, Rendall, Dooley and Ackford will not see another World Cup; but what they have established is the norm of fitness and dedication required. They have proved what is attainable and what can be achieved if the desire to succeed is translated into lonely hours of endeavour. For that they have to be admired. But I have to confess that when semi-final and final time came around I wanted Scotland and Australia to win. I'll be honest: I didn't want England to win against Italy, the USA, France or New Zealand.

Why? Because I knew what life would be like if England had won the World Cup. It isn't a sour note, but I'm sure that every Scotsman, Irishman and Welshman would agree that life would be intolerable with England at the helm of world rugby. It would also have concealed what we all know, but many of us have failed to recognise – that in terms of athleticism and ability to lift the game onto another plane we, and I mean the Five Nations countries, are more than a decade of thinking, planning and attitudes behind the Wallabies and New Zealand.

At least the Scots and the Irish could hold their heads high. I had fancied the Scots to win the World Cup, because to my mind they were a well balanced unit, and there are few back rows that are as unforgiving as Messrs Calder, White and Jeffrey. Gary Armstrong was enormous in every way, and to my mind the best scrum-half on view. You have to hand it to the Scots. The sound of "Flower of

Scotland" ringing around Murrayfield must have reminded a few Welsh players of how that kind of support can arouse and sustain passion. They were rarely found wanting in that department, and in the frenzied atmosphere of a World Cup, there wasn't a single Scot who didn't want to die for the cause. It was the same with the Irish against Australia.

Perhaps there were ability deficiencies in the Scots team. Doddie Weir's time will come again, to be a major force in the Five Nations when he fills out, and of course they will need to discover back row replacements fairly quickly. No one will be able to ignore Scotland, however, if they have Gavin Hastings on board. Again, here was an immense contribution from a player of class. I know he missed that kick against England, but who am I to say that these things don't happen?

The Finlay Calder tackle on the Irish full-back Jim Staples in the quarter-final, a tackle which had a crucial effect on the outcome, was the one blemish, in my view, on an otherwise impressive World Cup performance. Finlay should have been sent off for it. There were other incidents during the event which went unpunished, namely when I saw Peter Winterbottom apparently kick a French player. To my surprise Winterbottom was not punished by the referee nor was the incident commented on by the England management.

I have no time for players, no matter how intense the battle, who attempt to inflict serious injuries on their opponents. There were incidents of an ugly nature, and perhaps the least serious of these saw two men, Keenan of Western Samoa and Sporleder of Argentina, shown the way to the dressing room by referee Jim Fleming.

The disgraceful Dubroca incident dragged France's credibility into the gutter. Their performance in the battle of Paris did them no favours either, and I'm sure that Serge Blanco would want that game erased from such a marvellous career. Will he want to retire on such a discordant note, I wonder? In fairness England refused to be intimidated, and placed so much pressure on the French that they cracked and became boorishly ordinary. Whatever happened on the field was soon forgotten as Daniel Dubroca lost his cool by attacking the referee, David Bishop. My immediate reaction was incredulity, and then I thought: if that had been a Welshman, he would have been banned *sine die* before the crowd had departed from Parc des Princes. I have little doubt either that if a Welshman had used his boots in the same fashion as Peter Winterbottom it would have meant the guillotine. We have that capacity to attract condemnation, whereas others, it seems, have to be proved guilty before justice is done.

Apart from such unsavoury incidents – much of the trouble resulting from the referee's insistence on blowing up too early at the rucks – there were moments to inspire and performances to applaud.

At least Scotland achieved credibility. Had that kick from Gavin gone over against England in the semi-final, it could well have been a momentous tournament for them. To give due credit to England, they had done their homework on Scotland. If anything, the Scots at Murrayfield against the old enemy were a little below par when measured by the standards they had attained earlier on in the competition.

What of my own country? From time to time during the tournament I had been asked by TV AM and the *People* to contribute a few thoughts on the performance of the Welsh. I realised it would be difficult, because before the first ball had been struck, I knew what a struggle it would be for Ieuan Evans and the rest of the boys. The television and the newspaper commitment became something of a burden – not because of early hours or deadlines but because it was difficult to find something constructive to say or contribute to the Welsh cause.

When Alan Davies had been appointed coach with Robert Norster I had the feeling that no matter what would be done in the short space of time given to any "messiah", whoever he be, the task was impossible. The media latched on to Davies as a saviour, but he for his part made no promises, and in fairness wouldn't commit himself to the Welsh cause beyond the World Cup. I remember telling him, "I don't think you know what you've taken on."

Nothing was going to change from the Australian tour. There had been a certain amount of enthusiasm in the Wales performance against an uninterested French team to celebrate the opening of the new lights in Cardiff during September, but all the ills were there for those perceptive enough to see them – but not for the press, especially the Welsh press. They saw that performance at Cardiff Arms Park as a new beginning, or at least an improvement on the old. It was utter nonsense.

By the time the World Cup descended upon everyone, Wales were probably the worst prepared team of the tournament, whereas they had every incentive to be the best. They didn't have a pattern, there were grave fitness doubts about key players and Glyn Llewellyn broke a finger punching a student in a practice game! And in some cases there were summer beer guts which had not disappeared.

I have to admit that I was glad to be out of it. There wasn't a single regret. The predictable disaster came against Western Samoa, who had impressed everyone in training with their dedication and passing skills under the guidance of former New Zealand winger Brian Williams. Those who claimed that the team wasn't Western Samoan at all and that half the players played provincial rugby, missed the point. The Western Samoans play in New Zealand to achieve exposure to the demands of top-level rugby. Good luck to them – for my money, they were the team of the tournament. Could they tackle? I caught myself wincing on several occasions as players such as Lam, Bunce, Vaifele and Tagaloa went searching for moving Welsh tackle-bags. Here under the influential leadership of Peter Fatiolofa was a team full of pride and fervour. They had what Wales lacked.

It seemed that most of the participating teams knew what would be required of them. Italy, for instance had been trounced by New Zealand in the '87 World Cup, but here they were, vastly improved and with players like scrum-half Francescato and the towering locks Croci and Favaro audaciously challenging the All Blacks at Leicester. Brilliant stuff and they will be no easy prey for Wales. Canada, too, impressed me: the battle of the elements at

Lille, again against New Zealand in the quarter-final, saw the Canadians ferociously driving at their illustrious opponents. To have beaten Romania must have been sweet; even sweeter was that robust performance in the muddy fields of France.

For some – Argentina, Fiji, Japan, Zimbabwe, the United States and Romania – the tournament must have been a little disappointing. After all, it is a matter of peaking at the right time, achieving goals and attaining potential. If it was disappointing for them, despite individual displays of brilliance from the likes of Yoshida (Japan), Kevin Swords of the United States and Martin Teran of Argentina, for Wales it was nothing short of disaster.

To see the Welsh team run onto the field against Western Samoa filled me with dismay. We had known about the World Cup for four years. Whereas the Aussies and New Zealanders, and England too, had mapped out their campaigns on fitness, diets, training, media and game strategies for months before hand, Wales, it seemed to me, took to the field with more overweight and ill-prepared players than you saw in all the rest of the participating teams put together. Who did we think we were kidding? No Alan Davies, Ron Waldron, Tony Gray, John Ryan or John Bevan can produce results if the players are not fit enough to take on the opposition. I knew the score before the World Cup and it came as no surprise to see Wales make an early exit and suffer the indignity of having to travel to Milan or Bucharest in order to qualify in 1995.

My real concern was for some of the talented youngsters who would be watching such a disgraceful performance. The Welsh Under 21 and Under 19 team have had some measure of success and there is every reason to hope for something better in years to come. But whom will they take as their role models? For Welsh youngsters the role models should be players like Michael Jones, Willie Ofahengaue, Tim Horan, David Campese and Phillipe Sella. We have to adopt and attain targets set by others if we are going to achieve any kind of status in World terms; otherwise, the visits to Rovigo and Milan will be on a regular basis.

If there were any bright moments during the Welsh

World Cup disaster, one of them had to be the performance of the Llanelli flanker Emyr Lewis. At least here was a forward able to compete on level terms. Richard Webster did well enough in the early games and I thought Michael Rayer, the Cardiff full-back, took his place with a great deal of assurance. I don't understand at all why he was replaced by Anthony Clement for the final group game against Australia.

There were so many disappointments, and as the Welsh prayed for an unlikely Western Samoan 0 Argentina 3 score at Pontypridd which would have allowed them into the quarter-finals via the back door, the immensity of our problems was only just beginning to dawn upon most people. Not only were the players who had complained about the rigid training disciplines of Ron Waldron in Australia not good enough to share the stage with the semi-finalist countries, but I doubt if they were even on parity with Canada, Italy, Ireland and of course the French.

If the truth be told, their solitary win against Argentina by 16 points to seven, flattered the Welsh. If the Argentinian half-backs Camardon and Arbizu hadn't squandered so much possession, it might have proved to be another embarrassing episode. I take no pleasure in making such assertions, but the burden of the past few years' experiences has not been easy to shoulder, and I have nothing but contempt for those who have ignored or chosen to avoid the hard work necessary to achieve success. The Welsh selection relied on certain players who have contributed little at club, let alone at international, level. Certainly our forwards need to study the disciplined approach laid down by other countries towards weight training, fitness peaking and pace. They might find the language, graphs, diagrams and achievement programmes a little familiar: they've had them for years, but they've stayed in the kitbags!

It was so misguided of our press to latch onto Alan Davies as a saviour after the performance against the French. He could only achieve credibility with players who were dedicated enough. I didn't envy him his task, because

I knew that we had too many shirkers and too many players who had little to contribute.

To lose against Western Samoa was devastating, to have achieved a result against Argentina was gratifying; but the gap between ourselves and Australia was awesome. Australia could have rattled up another mammoth score against Wales. They were again scoring at will, and if Michael Lynagh hadn't had one of those days, when he seemed to be staging a psychological battle against the new World Cup rugby ball, the electronic scoreboard at the Arms Park might have fused.

What will happen now, I wonder? Alan Davies says he's been persuaded by Bob Norster to stay at the helm. I have no doubt of his credentials as a coach, but are they any better than those of Ron Waldron? Ron knew what was required before the World Cup, but the players chose to ignore him. I met him during the tournament as he was walking towards the stadium. The scars are visible enough, and he would have known better than anyone inside the Arms Park that without the dedication required to compete, we were second- or even third-raters. Perhaps now the clubs will realise that the onus is on them to instil that disciplined approach which we need at national level. I remember Lynn Davies, the Olympic gold medallist in the long jump, speaking at a forum shortly after the World Cup. He said that most minor club athletes were more dedicated than some of the Welsh players in the national squad. He was right, and what a condemnation of our attitudes!

Yet when the results don't come, whom will they blame? The pens will be sharpened and suddenly Alan Davies will be hauled in front of Denis Evans and told to go. It will not be Davies' fault, nor was it the fault of Waldron, Gray, Ryan or John Bevan. All those coaches were given players who were not worth the effort. How many of them train before work, during their lunch hours and after reaching home? It takes hard work, and if you don't put in that kind of effort, you can't expect to win. When Alan Phillips was booted out by the Cardiff committee, or whoever, he said that his players were not putting in the work required at top-class club level. He spoke the truth, but most of the Welsh squad for the World Cup was based on his club. Enough said. I do think that both Llanelli and Neath, two clubs with dedicated players who know the score, would have fared better than Wales in the World Cup. They might not have beaten the Australians, although the Stradey fans will argue the point, but both would have qualified for the latter stages of the competition.

That is perhaps enough of a tirade. I only hope that those who will in future achieve international status with Wales will do so with pride and the hard labour required. Watching the World Cup, sometimes at the venues, sometimes at home, it left me with a sense of pride in being part of such an exciting game. It came alive on the screen, and that gave a massive boost to its promotion. My only hope is that it doesn't attract the wrong kind of support.

At the opening game in Twickenham between England and New Zealand the crowd jeered kicks and booed the All Blacks. Not only that: when the young lads dressed in the colours of the participating teams took part in the opening ceremony, the crowd demonstrated against certain countries. It was shameful and disgusting. That was a marvellous moment for these youngsters, and for some yuppie types to think it jolly good sport to boo these rugby hopefuls doesn't say much for their mentality.

There is a danger that the game will attract the wrong kind of support. Goodness knows, there are enough filling the grounds at the moment who haven't a clue as to what is going on. I heard them during the World Cup, impressing their neighbours with name-dropping and referee-baiting. They are pathetic, and I wish they would stay at home and give their tickets to charity – or at least to someone who appreciates the game. It is this "I was there" mentality: I suppose Max Boyce should be thanked for that. No, sorry, Max, I didn't mean it! But I bet he's come across a few as well.

I don't understand why some people whistle and boo during kicks. It must give them some kind of demented pleasure, but it shows a lack of respect for the player: no matter where he comes from, every player deserves better than that. It happens at Cardiff and there is nothing that annoys me more than not giving a player, no matter which country or club he represents, every courtesy. I know it is asking a great deal from some of our supporters.

All this should not detract from the World Cup. Wherever it is held in 1995, it is now here to stay. It is a marvellous stage, and those who graced it in '91 will have memories to share for the rest of their lives. Personally I enjoyed being on the touchline, since there was so much to admire, so many impressive individuals; and those who returned home will now know what they have to beat. Australia were worthy champions and with players like Tim Horan, Jason Little, John Eales, Tony Daly, Ewan McKenzie, Phil Kearns, Tim Gavin, Troy Coker, Willie Ofahengaue, Rob Egerton and Martin Roebuck still around in '95 I can't wait for it to start again.

Who knows? A certain David Campese might be there as well!

International Career Record

Points: 304 (2 tries; 43 conversions; 70 penalites; 0 drop goals)

Played: 37 (won 16; drawn 1; lost 20)

Captain on ten occasions (won 1; drew 1; lost 8)

Paul Thorburn broke Dusty Hare's record for a Northern Hemisphere player with 70 penalties in tests as against Hare's 67.

His 37 caps are a Neath record.

When he reached 304 he had overtaken Gavin Hastings to become second highest test scorer in the Northern Hemisphere behind Mike Kiernan (Ireland) on 308. He only twice failed to score in the 37 tests.

Hastings has since regained the overall lead since Thorburn and Kiernan ceased playing test rugby. Thorburn still holds the Welsh record for points (304), penalties (70), conversions (43), points in a game (21 v Barbarians 1990), points in a championship season (52 in 1985–6) and penalties in a championship season (16 in 1985–6).

1985

3 points	v France	Lost 3–14	pen
13 points	v England	Won 24–15	3 pens, 2 cons
12 points	v Fiji	Won 40–3	2 pens, 3 cons

1986

11 points	v England	Lost 18–21	3 pens, con
15 points	v Scotland	Won 22–15	5 pens
11 points	v Ireland	Won 19–12	3 pens, con
15 points	v France	Lost 15–23	5 pens

1987

9 points	v France	Lost 9–16 *(Ret Injured)*	3 pens
3 points	v Ireland (WCup)	Won 13–6	pen
10 points	v Tonga (WCup)	Won 29–16	2 pens, 2 cons
8 points	v Canada (WCup)	Won 40–9	4 cons
4 points	v England (WCup)	Won 16–3	2 cons
2 points	v NZ (WCup)	Lost 6–49	con
10 points	v Aust (WCup)	Won 22–21	2 pens, 2 cons
14 points	v USA	Won 46–0	2 pens, 4 cons

1988

7 points	v Scotland	Won 25–20	pen, 2 cons
5 points	v Ireland	Won 12–9 *(Ret Injured)*	pen, con
5 points	v France	Lost 9–10	pen, con
8 points	v West Samoa	Won 28–6 *(Ret Injured)*	4 cons
5 points	v Romania	Lost 9–15 *(Replacement)*	pen, con

1989

0 points	v Scotland	Lost 7–23 (Capt)	NIL
9 points	v Ireland	Lost 13–19 (Capt)	3 pens
12 points	v France	Lost 12–31 (Capt)	4 pens
8 points	v England	Won 12–9 (Capt)	2 pens, con
9 points	v NZ	Lost 9–34	3 pens

1990

12 points	v France	Lost 19–29	4 pens
2 points	v England	Lost 6–34	con
5 points	v Scotland	Lost 9–13	pen, con
0 points	v Ireland	Lost 8–14	NIL
14 points	v Namibia(1)	Won 18–9	2 pens, 2 cons, try
15 points	v Namibia(2)	Won 34–30	3 pens, 3 cons
21 points	v Barbarians	Lost 24–31 (Capt)	5 pens, con, try

1991

3 points	v England	Lost 6–25 (Capt)	pen
8 points	v Scotland	Lost 12–32 (Capt) *(Ret Injured)*	2 pens, con
10 points	v Ireland	Drew 21–21 (Capt)	2 pens, 2 cons
3 points	v France *(non-champ)*	Lost 3–36 (Capt)	pen
3 points	v Australia	Lost 6–63 (Capt) *(Ret Injured)*	pen

183